中外文**稀有版本**文献

《家庭、私有制和国家的起源》

②

英文版

【德】弗里德里希·恩格斯 ◎ 著

《家庭、私有制和国家的起源》的出版与传播

（代序）

一 国外主要版本和传播情况

恩格斯的《家庭、私有制和国家的起源》（简称《起源》）先后出了六版，其中第二版和第三版是第一版的翻印，第五版和第六版是第四版的翻印。因此，在这里将着重介绍第一版和第四版的出版与传播情况。

（一）《起源》第一版的出版与传播

1.《起源》第一版的出版

1884年10月初，《起源》在瑞士苏黎世问世，署名弗里德里希·恩格斯，著者为第一版写了序言。《起源》之所以在瑞士苏黎世出版，而不是在德国出版，是因为当时德国正值反社会党人法时期，而《起源》又并非是一部单纯的学术著作，而是指导无产阶级革命的理论武器，因此在这样的背景下，如在德国出版《起源》，则很难不被查禁。关于这一点，恩格斯早在1884年4月26日给考茨基的信中写道："关于**专偶制**那一章，以及关于私有制是阶级矛盾的根源和破坏古代公社的杠杆的那最后一章，我根本**不可能**写得适合反社会党人法的要求。"因此，"写得好，就一定被查禁；写得坏，就会得到许可。可是按后一种

做法，我办不到"①。正是在这种背景下，《起源》第一版在瑞士出版。

2.《起源》第一版的传播

在《起源》写作过程中以及第一版出版后，纷纷有译者与恩格斯联系希望能够翻译《起源》，其中涉及意大利文译本、波兰文译本、罗马尼亚文译本、丹麦文译本、法文译本、英文译本和俄文译本等。

关于意大利文译本，意大利社会主义者帕斯夸勒·马尔提涅蒂曾经在1884年11月18日致信恩格斯，询问可否将他的两部著作——《起源》（马尔提涅蒂当时正在翻译这部著作）和《德国农民战争》合成一本书出版。② 针对马尔提涅蒂的提议，恩格斯回信表示："该书的题材和《起源》一书的题材毫无共同之处。因此……后一著作单独出版好，至于出版的方法，我完全听从您的决定。"③ 1885年4月11日前，马尔提涅蒂完成了《起源》的翻译工作，并将译稿寄给恩格斯。恩格斯在收到译稿后，于4月11日回信并对已读部分给予高度评价，恩格斯说："我给您写这几行字，仅仅是为了告诉您译稿④已经收到并且正在校阅。希望过十天半个月后，能将译稿连同我的意见和建议一起寄还。就我至今已经读了的那部分来看，我认为译得很好。"⑤ 由于在同一时间内，恩格斯还收到了一份《起源》的丹麦文译稿，同时恩格斯还要校阅《资本论》的英文译稿，因此直到1885年5月19日，恩格斯才将《起源》意大利文译稿校阅完并寄出。恩格斯在1885年5月19日致马尔提涅蒂的信中说："译稿和我的意见一并用挂号寄上。很遗憾，我没有很好掌握意大利文，不能更好地表述这些意见；我还是希望这些意见您都能懂得。使我惊奇的是，您从未在德国生活过，也没有在德国研究过语言，却那么好地转达了我的思想。我只发现有几个略语、俗语和成语译

---

① 《马克思恩格斯文集》第10卷，北京：人民出版社2009年版，第515—516页。
② 参见《马克思恩格斯全集》第36卷，北京：人民出版社1974年版，第754—755页，注释265。
③ 参见《马克思恩格斯全集》第36卷，北京：人民出版社1974年版，第263页。
④ 恩格斯《家庭、私有制和国家的起源》一书的意大利文译稿。——原编者注
⑤ 《马克思恩格斯全集》第36卷，北京：人民出版社1974年版，第293页。

《家庭、私有制和国家的起源》的出版与传播（代序）

错了；这些话对于一个不知道该国日常用语以至方言的人，是不能很好领会的，这些话无论在语法书上或词典里都是没有的。许多地方，只要您很好地领会了意思，我认为您可以译得更灵活、更大胆些。我担心，关于'马尔克'的那条注释不够明确。我认为应该刊印的只有这一条注释。其余的只是让您知道一下就行了。如您对这条注释发生什么怀疑，请告诉我，我打算改写。请原谅，校阅拖了很久。白天我忙于口授马克思的手稿，晚上也不总是有空的：在同一时间内，有人寄来了一份丹麦文译稿①要我校阅，更不要说《资本论》②的英文译稿了。"③ 1885年5月29日，意大利文版的《起源》已经在印刷中，恩格斯在给劳拉·拉法格的信中谈到了他对《起源》意大利文版的评价，即"译者做了他所能做的一切，某些地方确实译得很好。但是，不能期待一个在贝内万托自学德语的人，能把德国成语译成相应的意大利成语。我又不能改正这种缺点，因为我的意大利成语，不是意大利的，只是米兰的，而且这也差不多忘光了"④。1885年6月13日，意大利文版的《起源》应该已经出版，因此恩格斯致信马尔提涅蒂表示"请费神把您的译作寄**六本**给我——这就足够了"⑤。

关于波兰文译本，1884年8月12日，波兰社会党人、政论家玛丽亚·杨科夫斯卡娅-门德尔森（斯·列奥诺维奇）致信恩格斯，请求恩格斯允许将他的著作《起源》用波兰文发表。⑥ 为此，恩格斯于1884年8月中旬回信表示同意，但鉴于德国当时实行反社会党人法的恶劣氛围，所以希望波兰文版一定要在德文版之后出版。恩格斯在回信中说："同意。——我不得不向您提出的唯一的、但必须遵守的条件是：在全书用德文出版以前，**您什么也不要用波兰文发表**。在德国，此书将立即

---

① 弗·恩格斯《家庭、私有制和国家的起源》一书的丹麦文译稿。——原编者注
② 第一卷。——原编者注
③ 《马克思恩格斯全集》第36卷，北京：人民出版社1974年版，第315—316页。
④ 《马克思恩格斯全集》第36卷，北京：人民出版社1974年版，第318页。
⑤ 《马克思恩格斯全集》第36卷，北京：人民出版社1974年版，第323页。
⑥ 《马克思恩格斯全集》第36卷，北京：人民出版社1974年版，第746页，注释214。

被查禁，稍一不慎或过早透露，都会引起德国警方的注意，妨碍德文版的推销，甚至很可能使一大批书被没收。因此，收到此信，务请告知，并答应我：您一定履行这个遗憾的必要条件。"① 玛丽亚·杨科夫斯卡娅-门德尔森在接到恩格斯回信后，立即在8月20日致恩格斯的信中表示当天就着手翻译。但后来由于未可考证的原因，于1885年出版的波兰文本最终是由J.F.沃尔斯基翻译的。②

关于罗马尼亚文译本，恩格斯在1888年1月4日致罗马尼亚政论家、社会民主主义者若昂·纳杰日杰的信中有所谈及，他说："卡·考茨基……转给我几期《社会评论》和《现代人》，在这几期杂志中除其他材料外，还有您翻译的我的几篇著作，其中有《家庭……的起源》。请允许我对您的劳动表示衷心的感谢，您盛情地承担了这项工作，使这些著作能为罗马尼亚读者所了解。"③ 据考证，罗马尼亚文的《家庭、私有制和国家的起源》载于《现代人》杂志1885年第17—21期，1886年第22—24期。④

关于丹麦文译本，丹麦社会民主党人，社会民主党左派领袖格尔桑·特利尔承担了这项翻译工作。恩格斯在1885年2月底3月初校订了丹麦文部分译稿，认为译得很不错。⑤ 1885年4月23日，恩格斯在致维拉·伊万诺夫娜·查苏利奇的信中表示仍在校阅《起源》的意大利文译文和丹麦文译文，并阐发了"校订译文有时决不是一件多余的和轻而易举的工作"⑥ 的感叹。在1889年5月7日致保尔·拉法格的信

---

① 《马克思恩格斯全集》第36卷，北京：人民出版社1974年版，第201页。
② 参见《马克思恩格斯文集》第4卷，北京：人民出版社2009年版，第573页，注释17；《实现亡友的遗愿——〈家庭、私有制和国家的起源〉（1884年霍廷根—苏黎世版）的写作和流传情况》，胡慧琴译，载《马克思恩格斯列宁斯大林研究》1996年第2辑，原载《马克思恩格斯全集》历史考证版第1部分第29卷。
③ 《马克思恩格斯全集》第37卷，北京：人民出版社1971年版，第3页。
④ 参见《马克思恩格斯全集》第37卷，北京：人民出版社1971年版，第533页，注释1。
⑤ 参见《马克思恩格斯全集》第36卷，北京：人民出版社1974年版，第285页。
⑥ 参见《马克思恩格斯全集》第36卷，北京：人民出版社1974年版，第300页。

中，恩格斯再次说明，"特利尔是我的《家庭的起源》一书的译者"①。《起源》的丹麦文译本于1888年出版。

此外，《起源》的塞尔维亚文译本也于19世纪80年代末出版。②

关于法文译本，恩格斯早在写作《起源》的过程中，就预料到保尔·拉法格会想将《起源》翻译成法文，但是由于担心保尔·拉法格在翻译时的严谨性，因此迟迟没有答应。恩格斯的预料和担心可以从他的书信中表现出来。1884年5月26日，恩格斯致信劳拉·拉法格说："我预料，我的《家庭……的起源》出版后，保尔一定很想译它，因为那里面的东西正好是他所熟悉的；如果他要译的话，他必须把握住德文字的原意，而不要用他所喜欢赋予它们的意思，因为我根本不会有时间去加工。……我刚刚赶完的那本小册子，在一段时间内将是最后一本独立的著作。"③ 1884年9月13—15日，恩格斯在致爱德华·伯恩施坦的信中谈及拉法格翻译《起源》一事时说道："关于翻译我的小册子一事，你说得很好很对。但拉法格是**怎样**翻译的呢？他既不问自己的妻子，也不查词典，一切由他自己干，自作主张：这个德文词相当于那个法文词，而且还以赞赏自己杰作的心情把译稿寄给我。这样干，我自己也干得了。他当然希望马上担负起来，不过我们还得再看一看。"④ 后来，保·拉法格又表示打算把恩格斯的《起源》一书由意大利文转译为法文，这个打算也没有得到恩格斯的同意。⑤ 恩格斯在1885年5月29日致劳拉·拉法格的信中说明了他不同意的原因，即"意大利文版的《起源》也在印刷中。但是，你会立刻发现，不大可能从意大利文版译成法文。如果保尔只不过利用它来帮助理解原著，那是他的事情；不然的话，这只能使他搞出低劣的**复制本**和不好的改写本，而我根本不愿意拿出这样的本子给法国人看。译者做了他所能做的一切，某些地方

---

① 《马克思恩格斯全集》第37卷，北京：人民出版社1971年版，第189页。
② 《马克思恩格斯文集》第4卷，北京：人民出版社2009年版，第573页，注释17。
③ 《马克思恩格斯全集》第36卷，北京：人民出版社1974年版，第156页。
④ 《马克思恩格斯全集》第36卷，北京：人民出版社1974年版，第206页。
⑤ 《马克思恩格斯全集》第36卷，北京：人民出版社1974年版，第762页，注释316。

确实译得很好。但是，不能期待一个在贝内万托自学德语的人，能把德国成语译成相应的意大利成语。我又不能改正这种缺点，因为我的意大利成语，不是意大利的，只是米兰的，而且这也差不多忘光了"①。后来，福尔坦表示有兴趣将《起源》译成法文，并于1885年12月6日在致恩格斯的信中询问恩格斯，寄去一份试译稿。②1886年1月29日，恩格斯在致弗里德里希·阿道夫·左尔格的信中表示，当时他正在校订"《家庭的起源》——法文译稿"③。恩格斯这里提到的《起源》的法文译稿也许就是福尔坦的试译稿。但最终这项计划没能实现。1893年发行的第一次印刷的法译本是以《起源》的1891年第四版为依据的。④

关于英文译本，英国社会主义者、作家、政论家、马克思女儿爱琳娜的丈夫爱德华·艾威林博士和美国社会主义者弗洛伦斯·凯利-威士涅威茨基夫人都希望能够翻译。从恩格斯的相关书信来看，综合考虑《起源》翻译的难度、英美书报销售业的条件、美国工人运动的发展阶段及美国工人的需要、恩格斯著作的整体英译本情况等，恩格斯更倾向于由艾威林博士来翻译并在伦敦出版《起源》。恩格斯在1886年8月13—14日致弗洛伦斯·凯利-威士涅威茨基夫人的信中说："现在谈谈《起源》。这本东西比《状况》难译得多，每一页也许都要您付出较多的精力和时间。不过，如果我有时间校阅译文的话，这一点倒不会成为障碍，但您得付出必要的时间和精力，同时页边留宽一些，以便修改。这里还要注意一个情况。既然这本东西要用英文出版，那就应该在出版后使读者在普通的书店里就能买到。我估计《状况》就**不会**是这样。只要美国书报销售业条件同欧洲没有多大区别，书商就不会出售同他们

---

① 《马克思恩格斯全集》第36卷，北京：人民出版社1974年版，第318页。
② 《实现亡友的遗愿——〈家庭、私有制和国家的起源〉（1884年霍廷根—苏黎世版）的写作和流传情况》，胡慧琴译，载《马克思恩格斯列宁斯大林研究》1996年第2辑。原载《马克思恩格斯全集》历史考证版第1部分第29卷。
③ 《马克思恩格斯全集》第36卷，北京：人民出版社1974年版，第421页。
④ 参见《实现亡友的遗愿——〈家庭、私有制和国家的起源〉（1884年霍廷根—苏黎世版）的写作和流传情况》，胡慧琴译，载《马克思恩格斯列宁斯大林研究》1996年第2辑。原载《马克思恩格斯全集》历史考证版第1部分第29卷。

没有联系的工人政党的机构出版的东西。正因为此,宪章派和欧文派的出版物任何地方也没有保存下来,任何地方都无法找到,**甚至英国博物馆**都没有;正因为如此,我们德国党的所有书刊在书店里也买不到(早在反社会党人法以前很久就是这样),在党外,读者始终不知道这些书刊。有时候这种情况是无法预防的,但应该尽量避免。四十多年来,我在德国吃过这个苦头,现在我想使我的著作的英译本避免这种情况,这一点您是不会责备我的。英国的情况是:现在或者最近将来能为社会主义著作找到出版者,我不怀疑,明年我在这里能够出版英译本,并使译者得到稿费;此外,因为我早已答应艾威林博士翻译《发展》和《起源》(只要他自己能为自己的劳动搞到报酬的话),所以,要知道,美国版不由普通出版社出版,只会减少伦敦版由普通出版社出版并使读者到处都能买到的机会。此外,我并不认为,美国工人目前非需要这本书不可。《资本论》今年年底以前他们就可以买到,对他们来说这是最主要的。我的小册子作为通俗读物为实际宣传的目的服务,未必合适。在目前运动还不发展的阶段,我认为某些法国通俗著作倒是更合适些。……现在再来谈谈《起源》。我不想说,我已经无条件答应艾威林翻译这本东西,但是,如果译本要在**伦敦**出版的话,我认为我必须请他翻译。所以,最后如何处理,这在很大程度上要看您在美国出版这本东西的条件而定。……您自己知道,不仅这一本书,而且可能还有其他许多著作,我都有可能找一家资产阶级商业界中有名的出版社来出英文版,而且这样做有一个好处,就是翻译工作可以在这里进行(这会节省我很多时间),因此,在同意在美国单出版这一本小册子从而破坏整个事情以前,我得好好考虑考虑。同时,在目前美国反社会主义者的恐怖情况下,我怀疑您能找到一个愿意把自己的名字同社会主义著作联系在一起的职业出版者。……现在您可以相信,还要过一些时候美国工人**群众**才会开始**阅读**社会主义书刊。那些**已经在**阅读和将要阅读的人,可以找到足够的材料,他们最不会感到缺少《起源》这本书。盎格鲁撒克逊人的头脑,特别是在美国经过了一番非常讲究实际的发展,一点也不重视理论,除非是迫切的需要促使他们去接受理论,所以我的最大指望就是,我们的朋友们从自身错误的后果中得到的教训,会教育他们去钻研理论。"① 艾威林译的《家庭、私有制和国家的起源》一书在恩格斯在世时没有翻译出来。②

此外,恩格斯在1884年10月15日致卡尔·考茨基的信中还提道:"《起源》一书除要译成波兰文外,维·查苏利奇提出要译成俄文。"③ 但从后来的结果看,该计划没有成行,《起源》的俄文译本后是根据1891年第四版译出的。

综上所述,《起源》1884年霍廷根—苏黎世版出版后,分别出版了意大利文译本、波兰文译本、罗马尼亚文译本、丹麦文译本和塞尔维亚文译本,其中意大利文译本和丹麦文译本是由恩格斯亲自审定的。除此之外,《起源》的法文译本、英文译本和俄文译本也都在商谈之中,但由于种种原因,未能翻译出版。

(二)《起源》第四版的出版与传播

1.《起源》第四版对第一版的修订与补充

自《起源》初版问世至1891年的7年时间里,"对于原始家庭形式的认识,已经获得了很大的进展"④。1886年,俄国社会学家柯瓦列夫斯基和瑞士法学家霍伊斯勒分别发表了《原始法权·第一分册:氏族》和《德意志私法制度》;1888年,法国人种志学家勒土尔诺发表了《婚姻和家庭之进化》;1890年,俄国社会学家柯瓦列夫斯基和德国历史学家库诺夫分别发表了《家庭及所有制的起源和发展的概论》和

---

① 《马克思恩格斯全集》第36卷,北京:人民出版社1974年版,第493—495页。
② 《马克思恩格斯全集》第36卷,北京:人民出版社1974年版,第793页,注释493。
③ 《马克思恩格斯全集》第36卷,北京:人民出版社1974年版,第221页。
④ 《马克思恩格斯文集》第4卷,北京:人民出版社2009年版,第18页。

《古秘鲁的农村公社和马尔克公社》；1891年，芬兰社会学家韦斯特马克①发表了《人类婚姻史》；等等。因此，为了恰如其分地照顾到当时的科学状况，也为了弥补以前各版脱销的供不应求局面，恩格斯决定对《起源》第一版进行修订和补充。

关于《起源》第四版对第一版的修订和补充，恩格斯在1891年7月7日致劳拉·拉法格的信中指出："我正在结束《起源》第四版的修订工作。将有大量的重要补充，首先是写了一篇新序言（校样已寄给腊韦，该文可能在下期《新时代》上发表），其次是家庭一章有重大补充。"② 苏联学者文尼科夫曾对《起源》第四版对第一版的修订补充情况做过统计研究，他指出，这些修订和补充包括五种类型，共计144处。第一，文字上的修改，不改变本文基本的意义，有51处；第二，明确或发挥本文意义的修改和小的补充，有44处；第三，采用新的事实资料进一步发挥原来论点的，有20处；第四，原则性的修改和补充，有22处；第五，修改原文不确切的，有7处。按章节来看，第二章修改得最多，共75处，占了修改总数的一半以上。其次是第七章。修改不大的是第六、九章。几乎没有什么重大修改的是第一、三、四、五、八章。③

2.《起源》第四版的出版

恩格斯自1890年开始着手准备出版《起源》新版本。在可考证的相关书信中，恩格斯在1890年4月11日致卡尔·考茨基的信中首次谈及了出版《起源》新版本的事情，他说："昨天还收到了狄茨的来信，我……向他证实我同意……再版《起源》作为国际丛书中的一册。我

---

① 关于爱·韦斯特马克的名字，《马克思恩格斯文集》第4卷译为"爱·韦斯特马克"，《马克思恩格斯全集》第一版第39卷译为"爱·韦斯特马尔克"。本书中除部分直接引文中的名字仍采用"爱·韦斯特马尔克"之外，其他相关部分皆采用《马克思恩格斯文集》中的译法。
② 《马克思恩格斯全集》第38卷，北京：人民出版社1972年版，第126页。
③ 参阅文尼科夫：《〈家庭、私有制和国家的起源〉一书的第一版和第四版》，载《民族译丛》1956年第5期。

还答应作一些补充。"① 1890年5月20日，恩格斯已经开始为《起源》新版做资料方面的准备，他写信给弗·阿·左尔格，请求帮忙寻找摩尔根的最近著作——摩尔根的《美洲土著的住房和家庭生活》。② 恩格斯于1890年7月30日前收到了这本书。③

1891年底，经过修改和补充的《起源》第四版在斯图加特出版，虽然具体出版日期不详，但可断定是在1891年11月10日前出版的。因为恩格斯在1891年12月1日致劳·拉法格的信中问劳·拉法格："我三个多星期前寄给你的一本第四版《家庭的起源》，不知收到没有？我往欧洲寄了许多本，均未收到回音。寄往国外的书，哪怕少付半个便士的邮资，英国邮局都干脆予以没收，因此，我开始担心起来。"④

第四版出版后，又于1892年和1894年出版了第五版和第六版，这两版都是在第四版基础上翻印的。⑤

3.《起源》第四版的传播

《起源》第四版出版后，被译成法文（1893年）、保加利亚文（1893年）、西班牙文（1894年）、俄文（1894年）和英文（1902年）等，其中法译文由劳拉·拉法格校订，并经恩格斯审阅。⑥

《起源》第四版的法文版于1893年出版，可以肯定的是，该书是在1893年10月14日前出版的。因为在1893年10月14日恩格斯致劳拉·拉法格的信中，他说："我收到了三册《家庭的起源》的法译本。"⑦

《起源》的俄文译本于1894年在彼得堡出版，由德文第四版译出。

---

① 《马克思恩格斯全集》第37卷，北京：人民出版社1971年版，第374—375页。
② 《马克思恩格斯全集》第37卷，北京：人民出版社1971年版，第408页。
③ 《马克思恩格斯全集》第37卷，北京：人民出版社1971年版，第425页。
④ 《马克思恩格斯全集》第38卷，北京：人民出版社1972年版，第230页。
⑤ 参见《马克思恩格斯文集》第4卷，北京：人民出版社2009年版，第573页，注释17。
⑥ 参见《马克思恩格斯文集》第4卷，北京：人民出版社2009年版，第573页，注释17。
⑦ 《马克思恩格斯全集》第39卷，北京：人民出版社1974年版，第144页。

从恩格斯在 1894 年 6 月 1 日致尼古拉·弗兰策维奇·丹尼尔逊的信中可以看出，俄文译本的出版时间至少在 1894 年 6 月 1 日前，且恩格斯十分严谨地对已读译文给予了不错的评价，他说："《起源》的俄译本收到，十分感谢。就我读过的情况来看，我认为译文很好，对该书的书刊检查显然也是宽大的。"①

尽管在《起源》第一版出版后，恩格斯便同意由爱德华·艾威林博士将其翻译为英文版，但该译本在恩格斯在世时没有翻译出来。直到 1898 年艾威林去世，《起源》英文版也未能问世。因此，目前存在的《起源》英译本主要包括以下版本，且都根据《起源》第四版译出。第一，最早的《起源》英译本是由欧内斯特·翁特曼（Ernest Untermann）翻译，美国芝加哥查尔斯·H.克尔出版社 1902 年出版的版本。该版本主要内容包括第一版序言、第四版序言、正文，书前附译者序言。第二，1940 年，英国伦敦"劳伦斯—威沙特"出版公司出版由阿利克·韦斯特（Alick West）译，多娜·托尔（Dona Torr）校的译本。该译本由第一版序言、第四版序言、正文和附录——《新发现的群婚实例》构成，书前附出版者说明。该译本于 1941、1942、1943、1946、1972 年再版。第三，1942 年，美国纽约国际出版社出版《起源》英译本，未署译者，内容包括第一版序言、第四版序言、正文和附录——《新发现的群婚实例》。该版本于 1963、1970 年重印。1972 年，该出版社以 1942 年版译本为基础，同时依据《马克思恩格斯全集》德文版第 21 卷（Dietz Verlag, Berlin, 1962）中的德文原文对原译本进行了修订，出版了新版译本，即 1972 年第一版。该版主要内容仍为第一版序言、第四版序言、正文和附录——《新发现的群婚实例》，但在版权页增加了"出版者说明"，在书前附埃莉诺·伯克·利科克（Eleanor Burke Leacock）写的长达 67 页的导言，在书后附恩格斯的《劳动在从猿到人转变过程中的作用》及编者引言。从 1972 年版的"出版者说明"中可以

---

① 《马克思恩格斯全集》第 39 卷，北京：人民出版社 1974 年版。

得知，尽管该出版社在1942年版译本中并未署译者，但该译本的译者实为Aleck West，即1940年英国伦敦"劳伦斯—威沙特"出版公司的译本的译者。① 经笔者比对，1940年英国伦敦"劳伦斯—威沙特"出版公司译本与1942年美国纽约国际出版社译本确为同一译者的同一作品。第四，1940年，苏联莫斯科外文出版社出版《起源》英译本，未署译者，内容包括第一版序言、第四版序言、正文和附录——《新发现的群婚实例》。1948年，苏联莫斯科外文出版社出版修订本，同样未署译者，内容同样包括第一版序言、第四版序言、正文和附录——《新发现的群婚实例》，但是扉页有"出版者说明"，书前附联共（布）中央马克思恩格斯列宁研究院写的《序言》。在"出版者说明"中，出版者指出，"该版本依据恩格斯1891年的德文第四版进行了重新校订"。1948年版后来于1950、1952、1954、1959、1962、1968、1972、1977、1983、1985年重印。笔者目前只查阅到了1952、1954和1985年的重印本。1952年和1954年的重印本仍由苏联莫斯科外文出版社出版，书前不再附联共（布）中央马克思恩格斯列宁研究院写的《序言》。1985年的重印本则由进步出版社出版。第五，1972年，美国纽约寻路者出版社（Pathfinder Press）出版《起源》英译本，内容包括第一版序言、第四版序言、正文、附录——《新发现的群婚实例》《劳动在从猿到人转变过程中的作用》，书前附Evelyn Reed写的导言和关于翻译的说明。该译本于1973、1975、1976、1979、1983年重印。

此外，《起源》还收录在《马克思恩格斯全集》历史考证版（MEGA²）第I部分第29卷第125—271页；《马克思恩格斯全集》德文版第21卷第25—173页，俄文第一版第16卷（上）第7—153页，俄文第二版第21卷第23—178页，英文版第26卷第129—276页，日文版第21卷第25—178页；《马克思恩格斯选集》英文版第2卷第170—326页；等等。

---

① 区别仅在于1940年"劳伦斯—威沙特"版将译者印为Alick West，1972年国际出版社版在"出版者说明"中将译者印为Aleck West。

《关于原始家庭的历史》（即第四版序言）收录在《马克思恩格斯全集》历史考证版（MEGA²）第 I 部分第 29 卷第 132—144 页；《马克思恩格斯全集》德文版第 22 卷第 211—222 页，俄文第一版第 16 卷（下）第 117—128 页，俄文第二版第 21 卷第 214—225 页，日文版第 22 卷第 217—230 页；《马克思恩格斯选集》英文版第 2 卷第 172—184 页；等等。

二 国内主要版本和传播情况

《起源》一书是最早传入中国的恩格斯经典著作之一，在中国的翻译和传播经历了个人中文摘译本阶段、个人全译本阶段和新中国成立后有组织的集体翻译出版三个阶段。

（一）个人中文摘译本阶段

这一阶段的时间跨度为20世纪初至20年代末，期间的《起源》译本主要有两个特点：第一，翻译由个人完成；第二，译本并非全译本，而是摘译本，主要刊载在杂志刊物上。这一时期《起源》的主要摘译本如下：

1908年，中国出现了最早的《起源》摘译本。由志达摘译的《起源》第二章的若干段落，发表在《天义报》（日本东京）1908年2—5月第16—19卷合卷刊载的志达的《女子问题研究》一文中。该文将恩格斯这部著作译为《家族、私有财产及国家之起源》。

1920年10月，恽代英译述了恩格斯关于家庭的起源的观点，以《英哲尔士论家庭的起源》为题，发表在《东方杂志》第 17 卷第 19 号第 50—55 页和第 20 号第 67—71 页。这里的英哲尔士即指恩格斯，译述的主要内容为《起源》第四版序言和第二章"家庭"的部分内容，译述所依据的文本是《起源》英译本，这些信息在译文前的"译者志"中有所说明。恽代英在"译者志"中指出："英哲尔士（Frederick Engels）为马克斯（Karl Marx）的挚友，终身在宣传事业中联合努力。读马氏传的，无有不知他的。此篇节译其论家庭起源的意见。原书名'The Origin of Family Private Property and the State'。"① 另外，需要说明的是，这里之所以称恽代英"译述"的恩格斯论家庭的起源的意见，意在表明这种摘译不是按照原文逐段逐句翻译而成的，而是对部分段落内容的概述性翻译。

1922 年 1 月 15 日，邓中夏以笔名重远摘译的《起源》一书中关于国家的性质及其如何消亡的论述，刊载在他在《先驱》创刊号发表的题为《共产主义与无政府主义》的文章中。②

1923 年 8 月，熊得山摘译的《起源》第一章、第五章、第六章、第九章，分别以《历史以前底文化阶段》《国家的起源》《未开与文明》为名，发表在《今日》（北京）第 3 卷第 2 期第 76—81、30—46、57—75 页。③

（二）个人全译本阶段

这一阶段的时间跨度为 20 世纪 20 年代末至 50 年代中期，期间的《起源》译本也呈现出两个特点：第一，翻译仍由个人完成；第二，译本主要以全译本的形式出现。这一时期《起源》的主要译本如下：

1. 李膺扬译《起源》译本

该译本由李膺扬根据欧内斯特·翁特曼的英译本译出，并同时参照了西雅雄氏及田中九一氏根据德文版的二种日译本。它于 1929 年 6 月 10 日由新生命书局（上海）出版，书名译为《家族私有财产及国家之起源》，著者译为"恩格尔"，印有"社会科学名著译丛"字样，封面注明

---

① 《英哲尔士论家庭的起源》，恽代英译，载《东方杂志》第 17 卷第 19、20 号，1920 年 10 月。

② 参见《恩格斯和马克思主义》编写组编：《恩格斯和马克思主义》，北京：中国人民大学出版社 1985 年版，第 511 页。

③ 北京图书馆马列著作研究室编：《马克思恩格斯著作中译文综录》，北京：书目文献出版社 1983 年版，第 206 页。

《家庭、私有制和国家的起源》的出版与传播（代序）

"李膺扬译"，封底注明"校订者周佛海　译者李膺扬"，为竖排平装本。主要内容包括恩格斯写的第一版序言（1884年）、第四版序言（1891年）和正文，书前附出版者陶希圣于1929年6月14日写的序和译者序言。

出版者陶希圣在他写的序中介绍了《起源》的价值及出版《起源》的意旨，即"这本书的重要，是在以历史的唯物论来叙述民族学家所发见的材料。这本书的价值，是在民族学家所发见的事实能作历史的唯物论的证明。……本书是民族学开山巨著与历史唯物论交流之产物。我们介绍本书因此也有两方面的意义。第一在使读者得知历史唯物论的具体证据。第二在引起读者对民族学研究的端绪和兴趣"[①]。

译者在译者序言中简要介绍了《起源》写作的动因、基础、主要内容，以及该译本得以形成的文本依据，写道："本书有如著者在序言中所说，是恩格尔继承马克思在生前有志而未遂的工作所完成者，他根据关于这一问题的摩尔根之划时代的研究，加上自己的研究，并插入马克思的评注……把自蒙昧，野蛮以至文明的人类之生活之历史，由唯物史观的见地，简单地论述。我们从本书，不仅获得在历史研究方法上的一般的指示，更可看到人类原始生活中许多有趣味的事实，与三千年来我们文明基础的一夫一妻家族，私有财产制度及国家之沿革，还有锐利的马克思主义的对此之批评。要想知道马克思学派怎样地看男女关系，怎样地看国家，本书便是极有兴味而且重要的指针。……本书以 Ernest Untermann 的英译为底本；当翻译时，并参照西雅雄氏及田中九一氏根据德文版的二种日译本。"[②]

该译本在1929至1937年间，由新生命书局（上海）重印了7版，其中自第五版（1934年3月10日）起未署校者；在所有7版中，恩格斯都被译为"恩格尔"，全名被译为"菲特力克·恩格尔"。具体版本、形式如下：1930年3月30日，再版，印有"社会科学名著译丛"字

---

① 《家族私有财产及国家之起源》，李膺扬译，上海：新生命书局1929年版，第2—3页。
② 《家族私有财产及国家之起源》，李膺扬译，上海：新生命书局1929年版，第1—7页。

样，竖排平装本。1931年4月30日，第三版，印有"社会科学名著译丛"字样，竖排平装本。1932年7月23日，第四版，印有"社会科学名著译丛"字样，竖排平装本。1934年3月10日，第五版，印有"新生命高等文库"字样，封底无"校订者周佛海"字样，竖排平装本。1936年2月20日，第六版，印有"社会科学名著译丛"字样，竖排平装本。1937年5月5日，第七版，无"社会科学名著译丛"或"新生命高等文库"等字样，竖排平装本。

1938年6月，明华出版社重印该译本，封面书名同样译为《家族私有财产及国家之起源》，但著者译为"恩格斯"，全名译为"福里特里黑·恩格斯"，未署译者和校者，内容包括第一版序言、第四版序言和正文，同时删去了陶希圣的序和译者序言，竖排平装本。据笔者考证，明华出版社译本基本完全采用了前7版李膺扬的译本，区别仅在于两点：第一，将著者译为"恩格斯"。第二，去掉了部分译者注。例如，李膺扬译本"第一版序言"的第二段第一句话为"本书仅对我的故友（即马克思——译者注）所未能完成的工作，做成一点补充而已"①。明华出版社译本为"本书仅对我的故友所未能完成的工作，做成一点补充而已"②。

2. 未署译者、出版者、无出版时间等信息的译本

该译本为横排平装本，封面书名译为《家庭私产及国家的起源》，扉页书名为《家庭，私产及国家的起源》，封面著者译为"恩格思"，"第一版序言"和"第四版序言"末尾著者译为"法兰特里希·恩格斯"，无译者、出版者、出版时间等信息，内容由第一版序言、第四版序言和正文构成，封底有手写"一九三〇年 三、十六"字样。从该译本本身来看，可以确知该译本与李膺扬译本以及明华出版社基本重印的李膺扬译本不是一个译本，除此之外尽管无法获得关于该译本的其他确切信息，但是可以推断出以下内容：第一，该译本的出版时间在

---

① 《家族私有财产及国家之起源》，李膺扬译，上海：新生命书局1929年版，第2页。
② 《家族私有财产及国家之起源》，李膺扬译，上海：明华出版社1938年版，第1页。

1930年3月16日前。尽管无从考证该译本封底手写的时间点具体是购书者标注的购书时间抑或是出版时间抑或只是随手写的过去的一个时间点，但无论怎样，可以肯定的是，在1930年3月16日已经出现了该译本。第二，该译本可能是第一个将著者"恩格斯"译为"恩格斯"的译本。尽管该译本在封面将著者译为"恩格思"，但是在"第一版序言"和"第四版序言"末尾处则将著者译为"法兰特里希·恩格斯"。由于我们可以推断该译本在1930年3月16日前便已出现，早于1938年的明华出版社译本，因此据目前可考资料来看，该译本很可能是第一个将著者译为"恩格斯"的译本。第三，据目前可考资料来看，该译本很可能是第一个在书名中呈现出"家庭"字样而不是"家族"字样的译本。

3. 张仲实译《起源》译本

1939年，张仲实在盛世才反动统治下的新疆，不顾白色恐怖，根据莫斯科马克思恩格斯列宁学院院长亚多拉茨基重新校阅并编辑注释的《起源》俄译本，将《起源》译为中文。该译本于1941年2月由学术出版社（上海）出版，书名译为《家族私有财产及国家之起源》，著者译为"恩格斯"，全名译为"福里特里克·恩格斯"，印有"古典名著译丛"字样，主要内容为第一版序言、第四版序言、正文和附录——《新发现的群婚场合》，书前有译者序言，书中有编者注，竖排平装本。

张仲实的译本后来多次再版或重印，例如，1946年5月，生活书店（上海 重庆）版，书名译为《家族私有财产及国家的起源》，印有"世界学术名著译丛"字样，竖排平装本；1947年1月，生活书店（重庆 星加坡）重印，注明"胜利后第2版"，印有"世界学术名著译丛"字样，竖排平装本；1948年11月，光华书店版，印有"马列文库之六"字样，竖排平装本；1949年4月，新中国书局（印有"东北现名光华书店"字样）（长春）再版，印有"世界学术名著译丛"字样，竖排平装本；1949年4月，生活·读书·新知三联书店第一版，竖排平装本；1949年7月，新华书店（大连）重印，竖排平装本；1950年2

月，生活·读书·新知三联书店（上海）再版，书名为《家族、私有财产及国家的起源》，印有"马列主义理论丛书"字样，竖排平装本；1950年4月，生活·读书·新知三联书店（北京）第三版，印有"马列主义理论丛书"字样，竖排平装本；1950年10月，北京生活·读书·新知三联书店第五版，印有"马列主义理论丛书"字样，竖排平装本。

1954年，张仲实根据苏联国家政治书籍出版局1947年所出的《起源》俄文译本，对自己翻译的《家庭私有财产和国家的起源》一书进行了重新校订，补译了联共（布）中央马克思恩格斯列宁研究院序言一篇，并请人民大学研究部樊亢、谢家、王更生同志根据俄文译本，参考英、日译本校阅一遍，请中国科学院社会研究所汪敬虞同志根据英文译本校阅一遍，请北京大学东方语文系季羡林同志根据德文原文校订前半一部分，[①] 该校订本于1954年10月由人民出版社出版。书名改译为《家庭、私有制和国家的起源》，主要内容有第一版序言、第四版序言、正文、附录——《新发现的群婚实例》[②]，书前有联共（布）中央马克思恩格斯列宁研究院写的《序言》，书后有《译者后记》（写于1954年5月10日），书中有著者注、英文版编者注、俄文版编者注，本版为横排本，分精装、平装两种。

（三）有组织的集体翻译出版阶段

从20世纪初到1949年新中国成立前，马克思、恩格斯、列宁的许多重要著作都已经有了中文译本，但从整体上看，经典著作文本的中国化还存在大量问题，如经典作家的遗著中仍有大量文献尚未翻译介绍；已经出版的译本质量良莠不齐；各种译本译文风格不一，对经典作家的范畴、概念和术语译法不一；等等。在这种情况下，为了进一步提高译

---

① 参见《家庭、私有制和国家的起源》，张仲实译，北京：人民出版社1954年版，第176—177页。

② 1941年版译为《新发现的群婚场合》。

文质量，更全面地反映经典作家的全部理论，亟须成立一个专门机构来组织指导并从事经典著作文本的翻译工作。因此，新中国成立前夕，周恩来同志于1949年上半年起草了筹建中央俄文编译局的决定，中央俄文编译局于1949年6月正式成立。此后，中央又在中宣部设立了《斯大林全集》翻译室。1953年1月29日，经毛泽东同志亲自批示，中央决定将上述两个机构合并，成立中共中央马恩列斯著作编译局，"其任务是有系统地有计划地翻译马克思、恩格斯、列宁、斯大林的全部著作"①。中共中央编译局成立后，中国的马克思主义经典著作编译事业进入了一个有组织的集体翻译出版的新时代。借着这股东风，《起源》的翻译出版工作也进入了有组织的集体翻译出版的新阶段。

1954—1955年，中国派在苏联外国文书籍出版局工作的同志依据俄文版《马克思恩格斯文集》（两卷本）集体翻译出版了中文版《马克思恩格斯文选》（两卷本），《起源》被收入《马克思恩格斯文选》第2卷②第169—325页，内容包括第一版序言、第四版序言和正文，注明"集体翻译 唯真校订"。《马克思恩格斯文选》（两卷本）在《马克思恩格斯全集》出版之前被广泛使用，1958年和1963年，人民出版社先后两次重印。

1955年，中央编译局正式启动《马克思恩格斯全集》中文第一版的翻译工作，《马克思恩格斯全集》中文第一版依照收录《起源》正文和第一版序言的《马克思恩格斯全集》俄文第二版译出，同时参考了马克思的原著文字。③ 其中《家庭、私有制和国家的起源》正文和第一版序言被收入1965年9月出版的第21卷；第四版序言和"新发现的一

---

① 中央关于成立马恩列斯著作编译局与撤销中央俄文编译局的决定，参见《思想的历程》创作组编：《思想的历程：马克思主义在中国的百年传播》，北京：中央编译出版社2011年版，第107页。

② 《马克思恩格斯文选》（第2卷），莫斯科：外国文书籍出版局1955年版。

③ 参见《马克思恩格斯全集》第1卷，北京：人民出版社1956年版，扉页。说明：《马克思恩格斯全集》俄文第二版是根据苏联共产党中央委员会的决定，由苏共中央马克思列宁主义研究院编译，苏联国家政治书籍出版局于1955年开始出版的。

个群婚实例"被收入1965年5月出版的第22卷。联共（布）中央马克思恩格斯列宁研究院为《起源》写的《序言》未被收入《马克思恩格斯全集》中。关于中央编译局译校的《家庭、私有制和国家的起源》与以前译本的联系与区别，中央编译局在收录《起源》正文和第一版序言的《全集》第21卷中指出："'家庭、私有制和国家的起源'一书，是在人民出版社1961年单行本译文的基础上校订的，并由原译者张仲实同志审阅一遍"①；在收录《起源》第四版序言和"新发现的一个群婚实例"的《全集》第22卷中指出："关于原始家庭的历史（巴霍芬、麦克伦南、摩尔根）。'家庭、私有制和国家的起源'一书德文第四版序言"和"新发现的一个群婚实例"二文，是在1961年人民出版社出版的"家庭、私有制和国家的起源"一书（张仲实译）译文的基础上修订的。②

1966年3月，人民出版社出版《家庭、私有制和国家的起源》大16开本单行本，共两册，恩格斯的《新发现的一个群婚实例》作为附录收入本书，书后附注释151条，函装横排本。在该版的封底中，出版社对本单行本的文本来源及内容作了简要说明，指出："本书中第一版序言和正文部分的译文采自《马克思恩格斯全集》中文版第21卷，第四版序言和附录的译文采自《全集》中文版第22卷。这次排印大16开本时，由中共中央马克思恩格斯列宁斯大林著作编译局对译文作了一些修改。"③

1972年，为了适应读者学习马克思主义的需要，中央编译局编辑了4卷本《马克思恩格斯选集》，由人民出版社于1972年5月出版，封底注明"中共中央马克思恩格斯列宁斯大林著作编译局编"，其中《起源》被收入《选集》第4卷第1—175页，收入内容为第一版序言、第四版序言和正文，未附《新发现的一个群婚实例》。《选集》中《起源》

---

① 《马克思恩格斯全集》第21卷，北京：人民出版社1965年版，第827页。
② 参见《马克思恩格斯全集》第22卷，北京：人民出版社1965年版，第862页。
③ 恩格斯：《家庭、私有制和国家的起源》，北京：人民出版社1966年版，封底。

的译文采用人民出版社出版的《马克思恩格斯全集》的译文,经过了重新校订。①

1972年12月,人民出版社出版《家庭、私有制和国家的起源》单行本,注明"中共中央马克思恩格斯列宁斯大林著作编译局译",内容包括第一版序言、第四版序言、正文和附录《新发现的一个群婚实例》,书中有编者注,书后附注释和《族名索引》,横排平装本。

1995年,中央编译局编译的《马克思恩格斯选集》中文第二版由人民出版社出版发行,扉页注有"中共中央马克思恩格斯列宁斯大林著作编译局编译"。《选集》第二版的译文以第一版为基础,并依据1975年开始陆续出版的《马克思恩格斯全集》历史考证版,及《马克思恩格斯全集》德文版、英文版等进行了重新校订②,并对注释和索引进行了增补和修订。经过重新校订过的《家庭、私有制和国家的起源》被收入《选集》第二版第4卷第1—179页,收入内容为第一版序言、第四版序言、正文,未附《新发现的一个群婚实例》。

1999年,人民出版社出版了列入《马克思列宁主义文库》的《起源》单行本。

2009年,由中央编译局编译的《马克思恩格斯文集》10卷本由人民出版社出版发行,扉页注有"中共中央马克思恩格斯列宁斯大林著作编译局编译"。《文集》的译文根据《马克思恩格斯全集》历史考证版(MEGA²)、《马克思恩格斯全集》德文版(柏林)和《马克思恩格斯全集》英文版(莫斯科、伦敦、纽约)作了重新审核和修订。经过重新审核和修订的《起源》被收入《文集》第4卷第13—198页,内容包括第一版序言、第四版序言和正文,未收入附录《新发现的一个群婚实例》。

---

① 参见《马克思恩格斯选集》第1卷,北京:人民出版社1972年版,第1页;《马克思恩格斯全集》第21卷,北京:人民出版社1965年版,第27—203页;《马克思恩格斯全集》第22卷,北京:人民出版社1965年版,第246—259页;《马克思恩格斯选集》第4卷,北京:人民出版社1972年版,第1—175页。

② 参见韦建桦:《马克思主义理论建设的崭新成果——〈马克思恩格斯选集〉中文第2版简介》,载《马克思恩格斯研究》1995年第23期。

2012年，为了确保经典著作译文的统一性和准确性，由中央编译局编译的《马克思恩格斯选集》中文第三版由人民出版社出版发行，扉页印有"中共中央马克思恩格斯列宁斯大林著作编译局编译"字样，《选集》译文采用《马克思恩格斯文集》的译文，《起源》被收入《选集》第4卷第12—195页，内容包括第一版序言、第四版序言和正文，未收入附录《新发现的一个群婚实例》。

此外，民族出版社还根据中共中央马克思恩格斯列宁斯大林著作编译局的中译文翻译出版了蒙文版（1976年2月）、朝鲜文版（1976年12月）等民族文字的《起源》译本。新疆人民出版社出版了哈萨克文的《起源》译本（1959年版）。①

（本文来自2017年中央编译出版社出版的江洋所著《恩格斯〈家庭、私有制和国家的起源〉研究读本》有关内容。）

---

① 参见北京图书馆马列著作研究室编：《马克思恩格斯著作中译文综录》，北京：书目文献出版社1983年版，第208页。

THE ORIGIN OF THE FAMILY PRIVATE PROPERTY AND THE STATE

BY

FREDERICK ENGELS

TRANSLATED BY ERNEST UNTERMANN

CHICAGO
CHARLES H. KERR & COMPANY
CO-OPERATIVE

Copyright, 1902
By Charles H. Kerr & Company

TABLE OF CONTENTS

	Page.
Translator's Preface	5
Author's Prefaces	9-26
Prehistoric Stages	27
The Family	35
The Iroquois Gens	102
The Grecian Gens	120
Origin of the Attic State	131
Gens and State in Rome	145
The Gens Among Celts and Germans	158
The Rise of the State Among Germans	176
Barbarism and Civilization	191

TRANSLATOR'S PREFACE.

"An eternal being created human society as it is today, and submission to 'superiors' and 'authority' is imposed on the 'lower' classes by divine will." This suggestion, coming from pulpit, platform and press, has hypnotized the minds of men and proves to be one of the strongest pillars of exploitation. Scientific investigation has revealed long ago that human society is not cast in a stereotyped mould. As organic life on earth assumes different shapes, the result of a succession of chemical changes, so the group life of human beings develops different social institutions as a result of increasing control over environment, especially of production of food, clothing and shelter. Such is the message which the works of men like Bachofen, Morgan, Marx, Darwin, and others, brought to the human race. But this message never reached the great mass of humanity. In the United States the names of these men are practically unknown. Their books are either out of print, as is the case with the fundamental works of Morgan, or they are not translated into English. Only a few of them are accessible to a few individuals on the dusty shelves of some public libraries. Their message is dangerous to the existing order, and it will not do to give it publicity at a time when further intellectual progress of large bodies of men means the doom of the ruling class. The capitalist system has progressed so far, that all farther progress must bring danger to it and to those who are supreme through it.

But the forces, which have brought about the pres-

THE ORIGIN OF HE FAMILY

ent social order, continue their work regardless of the wishes of a few exploiters. A comprehensive work summarizing our present knowledge of the development of social institutions is, therefore, a timely contribution to socialist propaganda. In order to meet the requirements of socialists, such a summary must be written by a socialist. All the scientists who devoted themselves to the study of primeval society belonged to the privileged classes, and even the most radical of them, Lewis Morgan, was prevented by his environment from pointing out the one fact, the recognition of which distinguishes the socialist position from all others—THE EXISTENCE OF A CLASS STRUGGLE.

The strongest allusion to this fact is found in the following passage of "Ancient Society": "Property and office were the foundations upon which aristocracy planted itself. Whether this principle shall live or die has been one of the great problems with which modern society has been engaged. . . . As a question between equal rights and unequal rights, between equal laws and unequal laws, between the rights of wealth, of rank and of official position, and the power of justice and intelligence, there can be little doubt of the ultimate result" (page 551).

Yet Morgan held that "several thousand years have passed away without the overthrow of the privileged classes, excepting in the United States." But in the days of the trusts, of government by injunction, of sets of 400 with all the arrogance and exclusiveness of European nobility, of aristocratic branches of the Daughters of the Revolution, and other gifts of capitalist development, the modern American workingman will hardly share Morgan's optimistic view that there are no privileged classes in the United States. It must be admitted, however, that to this day Morgan's work is the most fundamental and exhaustive of

TRANSLATOR'S PREFACE

any written on the subject of ancient social development. Westermarck's "History of Human Marriage" treats the question mainly from the standpoint of Ethnology and Natural History. As a scientific treatise it is entirely inadequate, being simply a compilation of data from all parts of the world, arranged without the understanding of gentile organizations or of the materialistic conception of history, and used for wild speculations. Kovalevsky's argument turns on the proposition that the patriarchal household is a typical stage of society, intermediate between the matriarchal and monogamic family.

None of these men could discuss the matter from the proletarian point of view. For in order to do this, it is necessary to descend from the hills of class assumption into the valley of proletarian class-consciousness. This consciousness and the socialist mind are born together. The key to the philosophy of capitalism is the philosophy of socialism. With the rays of this searchlight, Engels exposed the pious "deceivers," property and the state, and their "lofty" ideal, covetousness. And the monogamic family, so far from being a divinely instituted "union of souls," is seen to be the product of a series of material and, in the last analysis, of the most sordid motives. But the ethics of property are worthy of a system of production that, in its final stage, shuts the overwhelming mass of longing humanity out from the happiness of home and family life, from all evolution to a higher individuality, and even drives progress back and forces millions of human beings into irrevocable degeneration.

The desire for a higher life cannot awake in a man, until he is thoroughly convinced that his present life is ugly, low, and capable of improvement by himself. The present little volume is especially adapted to assist the exploited of both sexes in recognizing the actual causes which brought about their present condition. By opening the eyes of the deluded throng and reducing the vaporings of their ignorant or selfish would-be leaders in politics and education to sober reality, it will show the way out of the darkness and mazes of slavish traditions into the light and freedom of a fuller life on earth.

These are the reasons for introducing this little volume to English speaking readers. Without any further apology, we leave them to its perusal and to their own conclusions.   ERNEST UNTERMANN.

Chicago, August, 1902.

AUTHOR'S PREFACE TO THE FIRST EDITION, 1884.

The following chapters are, in a certain sense, executing a bequest. It was no less a man than Karl Marx who had reserved to himself the privilege of displaying the results of Morgan's investigations in connection with his own materialistic conception of history—which I might call ours within certain limits. He wished thus to elucidate the full meaning of this conception. For in America, Morgan had, in a manner, discovered anew the materialistic conception of history, originated by Marx forty years ago. In comparing barbarism and civilization, he had arrived, in the main, at the same results as Marx. And just as "Capital" was zealously plagiarized and persistently passed over in silence by the professional economists in Germany, so Morgan's "Ancient Society"* was treated by the spokesmen of "prehistoric" science in England.

My work can offer only a meager substitute for that which my departed friend was not destined to accomplish. But in his copious extracts from Morgan, I have critical notes which I herewith reproduce as fully as feasible.

According to the materialistic conception, the decisive element of history is pre-eminently the production and reproduction of life and its material requirements. This implies, on the one hand, the production of the means of existence (food, clothing, shelter and

---

*Ancient Society or Researches in the Lines of Human Progress from Savagery, through Barbarism, to Civilization. By Lewis H. Morgan. Henry Holt & Co. 1877. The book, printed in America, was singularly difficult to obtain in London. The author died a few years ago.

THE ORIGIN OF THE FAMILY

the necessary tools); on the other hand, the generation of children, the propagation of the species. The social institutions, under which the people of a certain historical period and of a certain country are living, are dependent on these two forms of production; partly on the development of labor, partly on that of the family. The less labor is developed, and the less abundant the quantity of its production and, therefore, the wealth of society, the more society is seen to be under the domination of sexual ties. However, under this formation based on sexual ties, the productivity of labor is developed more and more. At the same time, private property and exchange, distinctions of wealth, exploitation of the labor power of others and, by this agency, the foundation of class antagonism, are formed. These new elements of society strive in the course of time to adapt the old state of society to the new conditions, until the impossibility of harmonizing these two at last leads to a complete revolution. The old form of society founded on sexual relations is abolished in the clash with the recently developed social classes. A new society steps into being, crystallized into the state. The units of the latter are no longer sexual, but local groups; a society in which family relations are entirely subordinated to property relations, thereby freely developing those class antagonisms and class struggles that make up the contents of all written history up to the present time.

Morgan deserves great credit for rediscovering and re-establishing in its main outlines this foundation of our written history, and of finding in the sexual organizations of the North American Indians the key that opens all the unfathomable riddles of most ancient Greek, Roman and German history. His book is not the work of a short day. For more than forty years he grappled with the subject, until he mas-

AUTHOR'S PREFACE

tered it fully. Therefore his work is one of the few epochal publications of our time.

In the following demonstrations, the reader will, on the whole, easily distinguish what originated with Morgan and what was added by myself. In the historical sections on Greece and Rome, I have not limited myself to Morgan's material, but have added as much as I could supply. The sections on Celts and Germans essentially belong to me. Morgan had only sources of minor quality at his disposal, and for German conditions—aside from Tacitus—only the worthless, unbridled falsifications of Freeman. The economic deductions, sufficient for Morgan's purpose, but wholly inadequate for mine, were treated anew by myself. And lastly I am, of course, responsible for all final conclusions, unless Morgan is expressly quoted.

FREDERICK ENGELS.

THE ORIGIN OF THE FAMILY

AUTHOR'S PREFACE TO THE FOURTH EDITION, 1891.

The first large editions of this work have been out of print for nearly six months, and the publisher has for some time requested of me the arrangement of a new edition. Urgent duties have hitherto prevented me. Seven years have passed, since the first edition made its appearance; during this time, the study of primeval forms of the family has made considerable progress. Hence it became necessary to apply diligently the improving and supplementing hand, more especially, as the proposed stereotyping of the present text will make further changes impossible for some time.

Consequently, I have subjected the whole text to a thorough revision and made a number of additions which, I hope, will give due recognition to the present stage of scientific progress. Furthermore, I give in the course of this preface a short synopsis of the history of the family as treated by various writers from Bachofen to Morgan. I am doing this mainly because the English prehistoric school, tinged with chauvinism, is continually doing its utmost to kill by its silence the revolution in primeval conceptions effected by Morgan's discoveries. At the same time this school is not at all backward in appropriating to its own use the results of Morgan's study. In certain other circles also this English example is unhappily followed rather extensively.

My work has been translated into different languages. First into Italian; L'origine della famiglia, della proprietà privata e dello stato, versione riveduta dall' autore, di Pasquale Martignetti; Benevento, 1885.

AUTHOR'S PREFACE

Then into Roumanian: Origina familei, proprietatei private si a statului, traducere de Ivan Nadejde, in the Jassy periodical "Contemporanul," September, 1885, to May, 1886. Furthermore into Danish: Familjens, Privatejendommens og Statens Oprindelse, Dansk, af Forfatteren gennemgaaet Udgave, besörget af Gerson Trier, Kjoebenhavn, 1888. A French translation by Henri Ravé, founded on the present German edition, is under the press.

Up to the beginning of the sixties, a history of the family cannot be spoken of. This branch of historical science was then entirely under the influence of the decalogue. The patriarchal form of the family, described more exhaustively by Moses than by anybody else, was not only, without further comment, considered as the most ancient, but also as identical with the family of our times. No historical development of the family was even recognized. At best it was admitted that a period of sexual license might have existed in primeval times.

To be sure, aside from monogamy, oriental polygamy and Indo-Tibethan polyandry were known; but these three forms could not be arranged in any historical order and stood side by side without any connection. That some nations of ancient history and some savage tribes of the present day did not trace their descent to the father, but to the mother, hence considered the female lineage as alone valid; that many nations of our time prohibit intermarrying inside of certain large groups, the extent of which was not yet ascertained and that this custom is found in all parts of the globe—these facts were known, indeed, and more examples were continually collected. But nobody knew how to make use of them. Even in E. B. Taylor's "Researches into the Early History of Mankind," etc. (1865), they are only mentioned as "queer customs" together with the usage of some savage tribes

THE ORIGIN OF THE FAMILY

to prohibit the touching of burning wood with iron tools, and similar religious absurdities.

This history of the family dates from 1861, the year of the publication of Bachofen's "Mutterrecht" (maternal law). Here the author makes the following propositions:

1. That in the beginning people lived in unrestricted sexual intercourse, which he dubs, not very felicitously, hetaerism.

2. That such an intercourse excludes any absolutely certain means of determining parentage; that consequently descent could only be traced by the female line in compliance with maternal law—and that this was universally practiced by all the nations of antiquity.

3. That consequently women as mothers, being the only well known parents of younger generations, received a high tribute of respect and deference, amounting to a complete women's rule (gynaicocracy), according to Bachofen's idea.

4. That the transition to monogamy, reserving a certain woman exclusively to one man, implied the violation of a primeval religious law (i. e., practically a violation of the customary right of all other men to the same woman), which violation had to be atoned for or its permission purchased by the surrender of the women to the public for a limited time.

Bachofen finds the proofs of these propositions in numerous quotations from ancient classics, collected with unusual diligence. The transition from "hetaerism" to monogamy and from maternal to paternal law is accomplished according to him—especially by the Greeks—through the evolution of religious ideas. New gods, the representatives of the new ideas, are added to the traditional group of gods, the representatives of old ideas; the latter are forced to the background more and more by the former. Ac-

AUTHOR'S PREFACE

cording to Bachofen, therefore, it is not the development of the actual conditions of life that has effected the historical changes in the relative social positions of man and wife, but the religious reflection of these conditions in the minds of men. Hence Bachofen represents the Oresteia of Aeschylos as the dramatic description of the fight between the vanishing maternal and the paternal law, rising and victorious during the time of the heroes.

Klytaemnestra has killed her husband Agamemnon on his return from the Trojan war for the sake of her lover Aegisthos; but Orestes, her son by Agamemnon, avenges the death of his father by killing his mother. Therefore he is persecuted by the Erinyes, the demonic protectors of maternal law, according to which the murder of a mother is the most horrible, inexpiable crime. But Apollo, who has instigated Orestes to this act by his oracle, and Athene, who is invoked as arbitrator—the two deities representing the new paternal order of things—protect him. Athene gives a hearing to both parties. The whole question is summarized in the ensuing debate between Orestes and the Erinyes. Orestes claims that Klytemnaestra has committed a twofold crime: by killing her husband she has killed his father. Why do the Erinyes persecute him and not her who is far more guilty?

The reply is striking:

"She was not related by blood to the man whom she slew."

The murder of a man not consanguineous, even though he be the husband of the murderess, is expiable, does not concern the Erinyes; it is only their duty to prosecute the murder of consanguineous relatives. According to maternal law, therefore, the murder of a mother is the most heinous and inexpiable crime. Now Apollo speaks in defense of Orestes. Athene then calls on the areopagites—the jurors of Athens—to

THE ORIGIN OF THE FAMILY

vote; the votes are even for acquittal and for condemnation. Thereupon Athene as president of the jury casts her vote in favor of Orestes and acquits him. Paternal law has gained a victory over maternal law, the deities of the "younger generation," as the Erinyes call them, vanquish the latter. These are finally persuaded to accept a new office under the new order of things.

This new, but decidedly accurate interpretation of the Oresteia is one of the most beautiful and best passages in the whole book, but it proves at the same time that Bachofen himself believes as much in the Erinyes, in Apollo and in Athene, as Aeschylos did in his day. He really believes, that they performed the miracle of securing the downfall of maternal law through paternal law during the time of the Greek heroes. That a similar conception, representing religion as the main lever of the world's history, must finally lead to sheer mysticism, is evident.

Therefore it is a troublesome and not always profitable task to work your way through the big volume of Bachofen. Still, all this does not curtail the value of his fundamental work. He was the first to replace the assumption of an unknown primeval condition of licentious sexual intercourse by the demonstration that ancient classical literature points out a multitude of traces proving the actual existence among Greeks and Asiatics of other sexual relations before monogamy. These relations not only permitted a man to have intercourse with several women, but also left a woman free to have sexual intercourse with several men without violating good morals. This custom did not disappear without leaving as a survival the form of a general surrender for a limited time by which women had to purchase the right of monogamy. Hence descent could originally only be traced by the female line, from mother to mother. The sole legality

AUTHOR'S PREFACE

of the female line was preserved far into the time of monogamy with assured, or at least acknowledged, paternity. Consequently, the original position of the mothers as the sole absolutely certain parents of their children secured for them and for all other women a higher social level than they have ever enjoyed since. Although Bachofen, biased by his mystic conceptions, did not formulate these propositions so clearly, still he proved their correctness. This was equivalent to a complete revolution in 1861.

Bachofen's big volume was written in German, i. e., in the language of a nation that cared less than any other of its time for the history of the present family. Therefore he remained unknown. The man next succeeding him in the same field made his appearance in 1865 without having ever heard of Bachofen.

This successor was J. F. McLennan, the direct opposite of his predecessor. Instead of the talented mystic, we have here the dry jurist; in place of the rank growth of poetical imagination, we find the plausible combinations of the pleading lawyer. McLennan finds among many savage, barbarian and even civilized people of ancient and modern times a type of marriage forcing the bride-groom, alone or in co-operation with his friends, to go through the form of a mock forcible abduction of the bride. This must needs be a survival of an earlier custom when men of one tribe actually secured their wives by forcible abduction from another tribe. How did this "robber marriage" originate? As long as the men could find women enough in their own tribe, there was no occasion for robbing. It so happens that we frequently find certain groups among undeveloped nations (which in 1865 were often considered identical with the tribes themselves), inside of which intermarrying was prohibited. In consequence the men (or women) of a certain group were forced to choose their wives (or husbands) outside of

THE ORIGIN OF THE FAMILY

their group. Other tribes again observe the custom of forcing their men to choose their women inside of their own group only. McLennan calls the first exogamous, the second endogamous, and construes forthwith a rigid contrast between exogamous and endogamous "tribes." And though his own investigation of exogamy makes it painfully obvious that this contrast in many, if not in most or even in all cases, exists in his own imagination only, he nevertheless makes it the basis of his entire theory. According to the latter, exogamous tribes can choose their women only from other tribes. And as in conformity with their savage state a condition of continual warfare existed among such tribes, women could only be secured by abduction.

McLennan further asks: Whence this custom of exogamy? The idea of consanguinity and rape could not have anything to do with it, since these conceptions were developed much later. But it was a widely spread custom among savages to kill female children immediately after their birth. This produced a surplus of males in such a tribe which naturally resulted in the condition where several men had one woman—polyandry. The next consequence was that the mother of a child could be ascertained, but not its father; hence: descent only traced by the female line and exclusion of male lineage—maternal law. And a second consequence of the scarcity of women in a certain tribe—a scarcity that was somwhat mitigated, but not relieved by polyandry—was precisely the forcible abduction of women from other tribes. "As exogamy and polyandry are referable to one and the same cause —a want of balance between the sexes—we are forced to regard all the exogamous races as having originally been polyandrous. . . . Therefore we must hold it to be beyond dispute that among exogamous races the

AUTHOR'S PREFACE

first system of kinship was that which recognized blood-ties through mothers only."*

It is the merit of McLennan to have pointed out the general extent and the great importance of what he calls exogamy. However, he has by no means discovered the fact of exogamous groups; neither did he understand their presence. Aside from earlier scattered notes of many observers—from which McLennan quoted—Latham had accurately and correctly described this institution among the Indian Magars* and stated that it was widespread and practiced in all parts of the globe. McLennan himself quotes this passage. As early as 1847, our friend Morgan had also pointed out and correctly described the same custom in his letters on the Iroquois (in the American Review) and in 1851 in "The League of the Iroquois." We shall see, how the lawyer's instinct of McLennan has introduced more disorder into this subject than the mystic imagination of Bachofen did into the field of maternal law.

It must be said to McLennan's credit that he recognized the custom of tracing decent by maternal law as primeval, although Bachofen has anticipated him in this respect. McLennan has admitted this later on. But here again he is not clear on the subject. He always speaks of "kinship through females only" and uses this expression, correctly applicable to former stages, in connection with later stages of development, when descent and heredity were still exclusively traced along female lines, but at the same time kinship on the male side began to be recognized and expressed. It is the narrow-mindedness of the jurist, establishing a fixed legal expression and employing it incessantly

---
*McLennan, Studies in Ancient History, 1886. Primitive Marriage, p. 124.
*Latham, Descriptive Ethnology, 1859.

THE ORIGIN OF THE FAMILY

to denote conditions to which it should no longer be applied.

In spite of its plausibility, McLennan's theory did not seem too well founded even in the eyes of its author. At least he finds it remarkable himself "that the form of capture is now most distinctly marked and impressive just among those races which have male kinship."*

And again: "It is a curious fact that nowhere now, that we are aware of, is infanticide a system where exogamy and the earliest form of kinship co-exists.**

Both these facts directly disprove his method of explanation, and he can only meet them with new and still more complicated hypotheses.

In spite of this, his theory found great approval and favor in England. Here McLennan was generally considered as the founder of the history of the family and as the first authority on this subject. His contrast of exogamous and endogamous "tribes" remained the recognized foundation of the customary views, however much single exceptions and modifications were admitted. This antithesis became the eye-flap that rendered impossible any free view of the field under investigation and, therefore, any decided progress. It is our duty to confront this overrating of McLennan, practised in England and copied elsewhere, with the fact that he has done more harm with his ill-conceived contrast of exogamous and endogamous tribes than he has done good by his investigations.

Moreover, in the course of time more and more facts became known that did not fit into his neat frame. McLennan knew only three forms of marriage: polygamy, polyandry and monogamy. But once attention had been directed to this point, then more and

---

*McLennan. Studies in Ancient History, 1886. Primitive Marriage. p. 140.
**Ibidem, p. 146.

AUTHOR'S PREFACE

more proofs were found that among undeveloped nations there were connubial forms in which a group of men possessed a group of women. Lubbock in his "Origin of Civilization" (1870) recognized this "communal marriage" as a historical fact.

Immediately after him, in 1871, Morgan appeared with fresh and, in many respects, conclusive material. He had convinced himself that the peculiar system of kinship in vogue among the Iroquois was common to all the aborigines of the United States, and practised all over the continent, although it was in direct contradiction with all the degrees of relation arising from the connubial system in practice there. He prevailed on the federal government to collect information on the systems of kinship of other nations by the help of question blanks and tables drawn up by himself. The answers brought the following results:

1. The kinship system of the American Indians is also in vogue in Asia, and in a somewhat modified form among numerous tribes of Africa and Australia.

2. This system finds a complete explanation in a certain form of communal marriage now in process of decline in Hawaii and some Australian islands.

3. By the side of this marital form, there is in practice on the same islands a system of kinship only explicable by a still more primeval and now extinct form of communal marriage.

The collected data and the conclusions of Morgan were published in his "Systems of Consanguinity and Affinity," 1871, and discussion transferred to a far more extensive field. Taking his departure from the system of affinity he reconstructed the corresponding forms of the family, thereby opening a new road to scientific investigation and extending the retrospective view into prehistoric periods of human life. Once this view gained recognition, then the frail structure of McLennan would vanish into thin air.

McLennan defended his theory in the new edition of "Primitive Marriage" (Studies in Ancient History, 1875). While he himself most artificially combines into a history of the family a number of hypotheses, he not only demands proofs from Lubbock and Morgan for every one of their propositions, but insists on proofs of such indisputable validity as is solely recognized in a Scotch court. And this is done by the same man who unhesitatingly concludes that the following people practiced polyandry: The Germans, on account of the intimate relation between uncle and nephew (mother's brother and sister's son); the Britons, because Cesar reports that the Britons have ten to twelve women in common; barbarians, because all other reports of the old writers on community of women are misinterpreted by him! One is reminded of a prosecuting attorney who takes all possible liberty in making up his case, but who demands the most formal and legally valid proof for every word of the lawyer for the defense.

He asserts that communal marriage is purely the outgrowth of imagination, and in so doing falls far behind Bachofen. He represents Morgan's systems of affinity as mere codes of conventional politeness, proven by the fact that Indians address also strangers, white people, as brother or father. This is like asserting that the terms father, mother, brother, sister are simply meaningless forms of address, because Catholic priests and abbesses are also addressed as father and mother, and monks and nuns, or even free-masons and members of English professional clubs in solemn session, as brother and sister. In short, McLennan's defense was extremely weak.

One point still remained that had not been attacked. The contrast of exogamous and endogamous tribes,

AUTHOR'S PREFACE

on which his whole system was founded, was not only left unchallenged, but was even generally regarded as the pivotal point of the entire history of the family. It was admitted that McLennan's attempt to explain this contrast was insufficient and in contradiction with the facts enumerated by himself. But the contrast itself, the existence of two diametrically opposed forms of independent and absolute groups, one of them marrying the women of its own group, the other strictly forbidding this habit, was considered irrefutable gospel. Compare e. g. Giraud-Teulon's "Origines de la famille" (1874) and even Lubbock's "Origin of Civilization" (4th edition, 1882).

At this point Morgan's main work, "Ancient Society" (1877), inserts its lever. It is this work on which the present volume is based. Here we find clearly demonstrated what was only dimly perceived by Morgan in 1871. There is no antithesis between endogamy and exogamy; no exogamous "tribes" have been found up to the present time. But at the time when communal marriage still existed—and in all probability it once existed everywhere—a tribe was subdivided into a number of groups—"gentes"—consanguineous on the mother's side, within which intermarrying was strictly forbidden. The men of a certain "gens," therefore, could choose their wives within the tribe, and did so as a rule, but had to choose them outside of the "gens." And while thus the "gens" was strictly exogamous, the tribe comprising an aggregate of "gentes" was equally endogamous. This fact gave the final blow to McLennan's artificial structure.

But Morgan did not rest here. The "gens" of the American Indians furthermore assisted him in gaining another important step in the field under investigation. He found that this "gens," organized in conformity with maternal law, was the original form out

THE ORIGIN OF THE FAMILY

of which later on the "gens" by paternal law developed, such as we find it among the civilized nations of antiquity. The Greek and Roman "gens," an unsolved riddle to all historians up to our time, found its explanation in the Indian "gens." A new foundation was discovered for the entire primeval history.

The repeated discovery that the original maternal "gens" was a preliminary stage of the paternal "gens" of civilized nations has the same signification for primeval history that Darwin's theory of evolution had for biology and Marx's theory of surplus value for political economy. Morgan was thereby enabled to sketch the outline of a history of the family, showing in bold strokes at least the classic stages of development, so far as the available material will at present permit such a thing. It is clearly obvious that this marks a new epoch in the treatment of primeval history. The maternal "gens" has become the pivot on which this whole science revolves. Since its discovery we know in what direction to continue our researches, what to investigate and how to arrange the results of our studies. In consequence, progress in this field is now much more rapid than before the publication of Morgan's book.

The discoveries of Morgan are now universally recognized, or rather appropriated, even by the archaeologists of England. But hardly one of them openly admits that we owe this revolution of thought to Morgan. His book is ignored in England as much as possible, and he himself is dismissed with condescending praise for the excellence of his former works. The details of his discussion are diligently criticised, but his really great discoveries are covered up obstinately. The original edition of "Ancient Society" is out of print; there is no paying market for a work of this kind in America; in England, it appears, the book was systematically suppressed, and the only

AUTHOR'S PREFACE

edition of this epochal work still circulating in the market is—the German translation.

Whence this reserve? We can hardly refrain from calling it a conspiracy to kill by silence, especially in view of the numerous meaningless and polite quotations and of other manifestations of fellowship in which the writings of our recognized archaeologists abound. Is it because Morgan is an American, and because it is rather hard on the English archaeologists to be dependent on two talented foreigners like Bachofen and Morgan for the outlines determining the arrangement and grouping of their material, in spite of all praiseworthy diligence in accumulating material. They could have borne with the German, but an American? In face of an American, every Englishman becomes patriotic. I have seen amusing illustrations of this fact in the United States. Moreover, it must be remembered that McLennan was, so to say, the official founder and leader of the English prehistoric school. It was almost a requirement of good prehistoric manners to refer in terms of highest admiration to his artificial construction of history leading from infanticide through polyandry and abduction to maternal law. The least doubt in the strictly independent existence of exogamous and endogamous tribes was considered a frivolous sacrilege. According to this view, Morgan, in reducing all these sacred dogmas to thin air, committed an act of wanton destruction. And worse still, his mere manner of reducing them sufficed to show their instability, so that the admirers of McLennan, who hitherto had been stumbling about helplessly between exogamy and endogamy, were almost forced to slap their foreheads and exclaim: "How silly of us, not to have found that out long ago!"

Just as if Morgan had not committed crimes enough against the official archaeologists to justify them in discarding all fair methods and assuming an attitude

THE ORIGIN OF THE FAMILY

of cool neglect, he persisted in filling their cup to overflowing. Not only does he criticise civilization, the society of production for profit, the fundamental form of human society, in a manner savoring of Fourier, but he also speaks of a future reorganization of society in language that Karl Marx might have used. Consequently, he receives his just deserts, when McLennan indignantly charges him with a profound antipathy against historical methods, and when Professor Giraud-Teulon of Geneva endorses the same view in 1884. For was not the same Professor Giraud-Teulon still wandering about aimlessly in the maze of McLennan's exogamy in 1874 (Origines de la famille)? And was it not Morgan who finally had to set him free?

It is not necessary to dwell in this preface on the other forms of progress which primeval history owes to Morgan. Reference to them will be found in the course of my work. During the fourteen years that have elapsed since the publication of his main work, the material contributing to the history of primeval society has been considerably enriched. Anthropologists, travelers and professional historians were joined by comparative jurists who added new matter and opened up new points of view. Here and there, some special hypothesis of Morgan has been shaken or even become obsolete. But in no instance has the new material led to a weakening of his leading propositions. The order he established in primeval history still holds good in its main outlines to this day. We may even say that this order receives recognition in the exact degree, in which the authorship of this great progress is concealed.

London, June 16th, 1891.

FREDERICK ENGELS.

THE ORIGIN OF THE FAMILY

CHAPTER I.

PREHISTORIC STAGES.

Morgan was the first to make an attempt at introducing a logical order into the history of primeval society. Until considerably more material is obtained, no further changes will be necessary and his arrangement will surely remain in force.

Of the three main epochs—savagery, barbarism and civilization—naturally only the first two and the transition to the third required his attention. He subdivided each of these into a lower, middle and higher stage, according to the progress in the production of the means of sustenance. His reason for doing so is that the degree of human supremacy over nature is conditioned on the ability to produce the necessities of life. For of all living beings, man alone has acquired an almost unlimited control over food production. All great epochs of human progress, according to Morgan, coincide more or less directly with times of greater abundance in the means that sustain life. The evolution of the family proceeds in the same measure without, however, offering equally convenient marks for sub-division.

I. SAVAGERY.

1. Lower Stage. Infancy of the human race. Human beings still dwelt in their original habitation, in tropical or subtropical forests. They lived at least part of the time in trees, for only in this way they

THE ORIGIN OF THE FAMILY

could escape the attacks of large beasts of prey and survive. Fruit, nuts, and roots served as food. The formation of articulated speech is the principal result of this period. Not a single one of all the nations that have become known in historic times dates back to this primeval stage.

Although the latter may extend over thousands of years, we have no means of proving its existence by direct evidence. But once the descent of man from the Animal Kingdom is acknowledged, the acceptance of this stage of transition becomes inevitable.

2. Middle Stage: Commencing with the utilization of fish (including crabs, mollusks and other aquatic animals) and the use of fire. Both these things belong together, because fish becomes thoroughly palatable by the help of fire only. With this new kind of food, human beings became completely independent of climate and locality. Following the course of rivers and coast lines, they could spread over the greater part of the earth even in the savage state. The so-called palaeolithic implements of the early stone age, made of rough, unsharpened stones, belong almost entirely to this period. Their wide distribution over all the continents testifies to the extent of these wanderings. The unceasing bent for discovery, together with the possession of fire gained by friction, created new products in the lately occupied regions. Such were farinaceous roots and tubers, baked in hot ashes or in baking pits (ground ovens). When the first weapons, club and spear, were invented, venison was occasionally added to the bill of fare. Nations subsisting exclusively by hunting, such as we sometimes find mentioned in books, have never existed; for the proceeds of hunting are too uncertain. In consequence of continued precariousness of the sources of sustenance, cannibalism, seems to arise at this stage. It continues in force for a long while. Even in our day, Australians

PREHISTORIC STAGES

and Polynesians still remain in this middle stage of savagery.

3. Higher Stage: Coming with the invention of bow and arrow, this stage makes venison a regular part of daily fare and hunting a normal occupation. Bow, arrow and cord represent a rather complicated instrument, the invention of which presupposes a long and accumulated experience and increased mental ability; incidentally they are conditioned on the acquaintance with a number of other inventions.

In comparing the nations that are familiar with the use of bow and arrow, but not yet with the art of pottery (from which Morgan dates the transition to barbarism), we find among them the beginnings of village settlements, a control of food production, wooden vessels and utensils, weaving of bast fibre by hand (without a loom), baskets made of bast or reeds, and sharpened (neolithic) stone implements. Generally fire and the stone ax have also furnished the dugout and, here and there, timbers and boards for house-building. All these improvements are found, e. g., among the American Indians of the Northwest, who use bow and arrows, but know nothing as yet about pottery. Bow and arrows were for the stage of savagery what the iron sword was for barbarism and the fire-arm for civilization; the weapon of supremacy.

II. BARBARISM.

1. Lower Stage. Dates from the introduction of the art of pottery. The latter is traceable in many cases, and probably attributable in all cases, to the custom of covering wooden or plaited vessels with clay in order to render them fire-proof. It did not take long to find out that moulded clay served the same purpose without a lining of other material.

Hitherto we could consider the course of evolution as being equally characteristic, in a general way, for

THE ORIGIN OF THE FAMILY

all the nations of a certain period, without reference to locality. But with the beginning of barbarism, we reach a stage where the difference in the natural resources of the two great bodies of land makes itself felt. The salient features of this stage of barbarism is the taming and raising of animals and the cultivation of plants. Now the eastern body of land, the so-called old world, contained nearly all the tamable animals and all the cultivable species of grain but one; while the western continent, America, possessed only one tamable mammal, the llama (even this only in a certain part of the South), and only one, although the best, species of grain: the corn. From now on, these different conditions of nature lead the population of each hemisphere along divergent roads, and the landmarks on the boundaries of the various stages differ in both cases.

2. Middle Stage. Commencing in the East with the domestication of animals, in the West with the cultivation and irrigation of foodplants; also with the use of adobes (bricks baked in the sun) and stones for buildings.

We begin in the West, because there this stage was never outgrown up to the time of the conquest by Europeans.

At the time of their discovery, the Indians in the lower stage of barbarism (all those living east of the Mississippi) carried on cultivation on a small scale in gardens. Corn, and perhaps also pumpkins, melons and other garden truck were raised. A very essential part of their sustenance was produced in this manner. They lived in wooden houses, in fortified villages. The tribes of the Northwest, especially those of the region along the Columbia river, were still in the higher stage of savagery, ignorant of pottery and of any cultivation of plants whatever. But the so-called Pueblo Indians in New Mexico, the Mexicans, Central-Ameri-

PREHISTORIC STAGES

cans and Peruvians, were in the middle-stage of barbarism. They lived in fortlike houses of adobe or stone, cultivated corn and other plants suitable to various conditions of localities and climate in artificially irrigated gardens that represented the main source of nourishment, and even kept a few tamed animals—the Mexicans the turkey and other birds, the Peruvians the llama. Furthermore they were familiar with the use of metals—iron excepted, and for this reason they could not get along yet without stone weapons and stone implements. The conquest by the Spaniards cut short all further independent development.

In the East, the middle stage of barbarism began with the taming of milk and meat producing animals, while the cultivation of plants seems to have remained unknown far into this period. It appears that the taming and raising of animals and the formation of large herds gave rise to the separation of Aryans and Semites from the rest of the barbarians. Names of animals are still common to the languages of European and Asian Aryans, while this is almost never the case with the names of cultivated plants.

In suitable localities, the formation of herds led to a nomadic life, as with the Semites in the grassy plains of the Euphrates and Tigris, the Aryans in the plains of India, of the Oxus, Jaxartes, Don and Dnieper. Along the borders of such pasture lands, the taming of animals must have been accomplished first. But later generations conceived the mistaken idea that the nomadic tribes had their origin in regions supposed to be the cradle of humanity, while in reality their savage ancestors and even people in the lower stage of barbarism would have found these regions almost unfit for habitation. On the other hand, once these barbarians of the middle stage were accustomed to nomadic life, nothing could have induced them to

THE ORIGIN OF THE FAMILY

return voluntarily from the grassy river plains to the forests that had been the home of their ancestors. Even when Semites and Aryans were forced further to the North and West, it was impossible for them to occupy the forest regions of Western Asia and Europe, until they were enabled by agriculture to feed their animals on this less favorable soil and especially to maintain them during the winter. It is more than probable that the cultivation of grain was due primarily to the demand for stock feed, and became an important factor of human sustenance at a later period.

The superior development of Aryans and Semites is, perhaps, attributable to the copious meat and milk diet of both races, more especially to the favorable influence of such food on the growth of children. As a matter of fact, the Pueblo Indians of New Mexico who live on an almost purely vegetarian diet, have a smaller brain than the Indians in the lower stage of barbarism who eat more meat and fish. At any rate, cannibalism gradually disappears at this stage and is maintained only as a religious observance or, what is here nearly identical, as a magic remedy.*

3. Higher Stage. Beginning with the melting of iron ore and merging into civilization by the inven-

---

Translator's note.

*Advocates of vegetarianism may, of course, challenge this statement and show that all the testimony of anthropology is not in favor of the meat-eaters. It must also be admitted that diet is not the only essential factor in environment which influences the development of races. And there is no conclusive evidence to prove the absolute superiority of one diet over another. Neither have we any proofs that cannibalism ever was in general practice. It rather seems to have been confined to limited groups of people in especially ill-favored localities or to times of great scarcity of food. Hence we can neither refer to cannibalism as a typical stage in human history, nor are we obliged to accept the vegetarian hypothesis of a transition from a meat diet to a plant diet as a condition sine qua non of higher human development.

PREHISTORIC STAGES

tion of letter script and its utilization for writing records. This stage which is passed independently only on the Eastern Hemisphere, is richer in improvements of production than all preceding stages together. It is the stage of the Greek heroes, the Italian tribes shortly before the foundation of Rome, the Germans of Tacitus, the Norsemen of the Viking age.

We are here confronted for the first time with the iron ploughshare drawn by animals, rendering possible agriculture on a large scale, in fields, and hence a practically unlimited increase in the production of food for the time being. The next consequence is the clearing of forests and their transformation into arable land and meadows—which process, however, could not be continued on a larger scale without the help of the iron ax and the iron spade. Naturally, these improvements brought a more rapid increase of population and a concentration of numbers into a small area. Before the time of field cultivation a combination of half a million of people under one central management could have been possible only under exceptionably favorable conditions; most likely this was never the case.

The greatest attainments of the higher stage of barbarism are presented in Homer's poems, especially in the Iliad. Improved iron tools; the bellows; the handmill; the potter's wheel; the preparation of oil and wine; a well developed fashioning of metals verging on artisanship; the wagon and chariot; ship-building with beams and boards; the beginning of artistic architecture; towns surrounded by walls with turrets and battlements; the Homeric epos and the entire mythology—these are the principal bequests transmitted by the Greeks from barbarism to civilization. In comparing these attainments with the description given by Cesar or even Tacitus of Germans, who were in

THE ORIGIN OF THE FAMILY

the beginning of the same stage of evolution which the Greeks were preparing to leave for a higher one, we perceive the wealth of productive development comprised in the higher stage of barbarism.

The sketch which I have here produced after Morgan of the evolution of the human race through savagery and barbarism to the beginning of civilization is even now rich in new outlines. More still, these outlines are incontrovertible, because traced directly from production. Nevertheless, this sketch will appear faint and meagre in comparison to the panorama unrolled to our view at the end of our pilgrimage. Not until then will it be possible to show in their true light both the transition from barbarianism to civilization and the striking contrast between them. For the present we can summarize Morgan's arrangement in the following manner: Savagery—time of predominating appropriation of finished natural products; human ingenuity invents mainly tools useful in assisting this appropriation. Barbarism—time of acquiring the knowledge of cattle raising, of agriculture and of new methods for increasing the productivity of nature by human agency. Civilization: time of learning a wider utilization of natural products, of manufacturing and of art.

CHAPTER II.

THE FAMILY.

Morgan, who spent the greater part of his life among the Iroquois in the State of New York and who had been adopted into one of their tribes, the Senecas, found among them a system of relationship that was in contradiction with their actual family relations. Among them existed what Morgan terms the syndyasmian or pairing family, a monogamous state easily dissolved by either side. The offspring of such a couple was identified and acknowledged by all the world. There could be no doubt to whom to apply the terms father, mother, son, daughter, brother, sister. But the actual use of these words was not in keeping with their fundamental meaning. For the Iroquois addresses as sons and daughters not only his own children, but also those of his brothers; and he is called father by all of them. But the children of his sisters he calls nephews and nieces, and they call him uncle. Vice versa, an Iroquois woman calls her own children as well as those of her sisters sons and daughters and is addressed as mother by them. But the children of her brothers are called nephews and nieces, and they call her aunt. In the same way, the children of brothers call one another brothers and sisters, and so do the children of sisters. But the children of a sister call those of her brother cousins, and vice versa. And these are not simply meaningless terms, but expressions of actually existing conceptions of proximity and remoteness, equality or inequality of consanguinity.

These conceptions serve as the fundament of a perfectly elaborated system of relationship, capable of

THE ORIGIN OF THE FAMILY

expressing several hundred different relations of a single individual. More still, this system is not only fully accepted by all American Indians—no exception has been found so far—but it is also in use with hardly any modifications among the original inhabitants of India, among the Dravidian tribes of the Dekan and the Gaura tribes of Hindostan.

The terms of relationship used by the Tamils of Southern India and by the Seneca-Iroquois of New York State are to this day identical for more than two hundred different family relations. And among these East Indian tribes also, as among all American Indians, the relations arising out of the prevailing form of the family are not in keeping with the system of kinship.

How can this be explained? In view of the important role played by kinship in the social order of all the savage and barbarian races, the significance of such a widespread system cannot be obliterated by phrases.

A system that is generally accepted in America, that also exists in Asia among people of entirely different races, that is frequently found in a more or less modified form all over Africa and Australia, such a system requires a historical explanation and cannot be talked down, as was attempted, e. g., by McLennan. The terms father, child, brother, sister are more than mere honorary titles; they carry in their wake certain well-defined and very serious obligations, the aggregate of which comprises a very essential part of the social constitution of those nations. And the explanation was found. In the Sandwich Islands (Hawaii) there existed up to the first half of the nineteenth century a family form producing just such fathers and mothers, brothers and sisters, uncles and aunts, nephews and nieces, as the old Indo-American system of kinship. But how remarkable! The Hawaiian system of kinship again did not agree with the family form

THE FAMILY

actually prevailing there. For there all the children of brothers and sisters, without any exception, are considered brothers and sisters, and regarded as the common children not only of their mother or her sisters, or their father and his brothers, but of all the brothers and sisters of their parents without distinction. While thus the American system of kinship presupposes an obsolete primitive form of the family, which is still actually existing in Hawaii, the Hawaiian system on the other hand points to a still more primitive form of the family, the actual existence of which cannot be proved any more, but which must have existed, because otherwise such a system of kinship could not have arisen. According to Morgan, the family is the active element; it is never stationary, but in progression from a lower to a higher form in the same measure in which society develops from a lower to a higher stage. But the systems of kinship are passive. Only in long intervals they register the progress made by the family in course of time, and only then are they radically changed, when the family has done so. "And," adds Marx, "it is the same with political, juridical, religious and philosophical systems in general." While the family keeps on growing, the system of kinship becomes ossified. The latter continues in this state and the family grows beyond it. With the same certainty which enabled Cuvier to conclude from some bones of Marsupialia found near Paris that extinct marsupialia had lived there, with this same certainty may we conclude from a system of kinship transmitted by history that the extinct form of the family corresponding to this system was once in existence.

The systems of kinship and forms of the family just mentioned differ from the present systems in that every child has several fathers and mothers. Under the American system to which the Hawaiian system

THE ORIGIN OF THE FAMILY

corresponds, brother and sister cannot be father and mother of the same child; but the Hawaiian system presupposes a family, in which, on the contrary, this was the rule. We are here confronted by a series of family forms that are in direct contradiction with those that were currently regarded as alone prevailing. The conventional conception knows only monogamy, furthermore polygamy of one man, eventually also polyandry of one woman. But it passes in silence, as is meet for a moralizing philistine, that the practice silently but without compunction supersedes these barriers sanctioned officially by society. The study of primeval history, however, shows us conditions, where men practiced polygamy and women at the same time polyandry, so that their children were considered common to all; conditions that up to their final transition into monogamy underwent a whole series of modifications. These modifications slowly and gradually contract the circle comprised by the common tie of marriage until only the single couple remains which prevails to-day.

In thus constructing backward the history of the family, Morgan, in harmony with the majority of his colleagues, arrives at a primeval condition, where unrestricted sexual intercourse existed within a tribe, so that every woman belonged to every man, and vice versa.

Much has been said about this primeval state of affairs since the eighteenth century, but only in general commonplaces. It is one of Bachofen's great merits to have taken the subject seriously and to have searched for traces of this state in historical and religious traditions. To-day we know that these traces, found by him, do not lead back to a stage of unlimited sexual intercourse, but to a much later form, the group marriage. The primeval stage, if it really ever existed, belongs to so remote a period, that we can hardly

THE FAMILY

expect to find direct proofs of its former existence among these social fossils, backward savages. Bachofen's merit consists in having brought this question to the fore.*

It has lately become a fashion to deny the existence of this early stage of human sex life, in order to spare us this "shame." Apart from the absence of all direct proof, the example of the rest of animal life is invoked. From the latter, Letourneau (Evolution du mariage et de la famille, 1888) quoted numerous facts, alleged to prove that among animals also an absolutely unlimited sexual intercourse belongs to a lower stage. But I can only conclude from all these facts that they prove absolutely nothing for man and the primeval conditions of his life. The mating of vertebrates for a lengthy term is sufficiently explained by physiological causes, e. g., among birds by the helplessness of the female during brooding time. Examples of faithful monogamy among birds do not furnish any proofs for men, for we are not descended from birds.

And if strict monogamy is the height of virtue, then the palm belongs to the tapeworm that carries a complete male and female sexual apparatus in each of its 50 to 200 sections and passes its whole lifetime in fertilizing itself in every one of its sections. But if we confine ourselves to mammals, we find all forms of sexual intercourse, license, suggestions of group mar-

---

Author's note.
*How little Bachofen understood what he had discovered, or rather guessed, is proved by the term "hetaerism," which he applies to this primeval stage. Hetaerism designated among the Greeks an intercourse of men, single or living in monogamy, with unmarried women. It always presupposes the existence of a well defined form of marriage, outside of which this intercourse takes place, and includes the possibility of prostitution. In another sense this word was never used, and I use it in this sense with Morgan. Bachofen's very important discoveries are everywhere mystified in the extreme by his idea that the historical relations of man and wife have their source in the religious conceptions of a certain period, not in the economic conditions of life.

THE ORIGIN OF THE FAMILY

riage, polygamy and monogamy. Only polyandry is missing;* that could be accomplished by men only. Even our next relations, the quadrumana, exhibit all possible differences in the grouping of males and females. And if we draw the line still closer and consider only the four anthropoid apes, Letourneau can only tell us, that they are now monogamous, now polygamous; while Saussure contends according to Giraud-Teulon that they are monogamous. The recent contentions of Westermarck* in regard to monogamy among anthropoid apes are far from proving anything. In short, the information is such that honest Letourneau admits: "There exists no strict relation at all between the degree of intellectual development and the form of sexual intercourse among mammals." And Espinas says frankly:* "The herd is the highest social group found among animals. It seems to be composed of families, but from the outset the family and the herd are antagonistic; they develop in directly opposite ratio."

It is evident from the above that we know next to nothing of the family and other social groups of anthropoid apes; the reports are directly contradictory. How full of contradiction, how much in need of critical scrutiny and research are the reports even on savage human tribes! But monkey tribes are far more difficult to observe than human tribes. For the present, therefore, we must decline all final conclusions from such absolutely unreliable reports.

Translator's note.

*The female of the European cuckoo (cuculus canorus) keeps intercourse with several males in different districts during the same season. Still, this is far from the human polyandry, in which the men and one women all live together in the same place, the men mutually tolerating one another, which male cuckoos do not.

*Westermarck, The History of Human Marriage, London, 1891.

*Espinas, Des Societes Animales, 1877.

THE FAMILY

The quotation from Espinas, however, offers a better clue. Among higher animals, the herd and family are not supplements of one another, but antitheses. Espinas demonstrates very nicely, how the jealousy of the males loosens or temporarily dissolves every herd during mating time. "Where the family is closely organized, herds are formed only in exceptional cases. But wherever free sexual intercourse or polygamy are existing, the herd appears almost spontaneously. . . . In order that a herd may form, family ties must be loosened and the individual be free. For this reason we so rarely find organized herds among birds. . . . Among mammals, however, we find groups organized after a fashion, just because here the individual is not merged in the family. . . . The rising sense of cohesion in a herd cannot, therefore, have a greater enemy than the consciousness of family ties. Let us not shrink from pronouncing it: the development of a higher form of society than the family can be due only to the fact that it admitted families which had undergone a thorough change. This does not exclude the possibility that these same families were thus enabled to reorganize later on under infinitely more favorable circumstances."*

It becomes apparent from this, that animal societies may indeed have a certain value in drawing conclusions in regard to human life—but only negatively. The higher vertebrate knows, so far as we may ascertain, only two forms of the family: polygamy or pairs. In both of them there is only one grown male, only one husband. The jealousy of the male, at the same time tie and limit of the family, creates an opposition between the animal family and the herd. The latter, a higher social form, is here rendered impossible, there loosened or dissolved during mating time, and at

---
*Espinas, l. c., quoted by Giraud-Teulon. Origines du mariage et de la famille, 1884, p. 518-20.

THE ORIGIN OF THE FAMILY

best hindered in its development by the jealousy of the male. This in itself is sufficient proof that the animal family and primeval human society are irreconcilable; that ancient man, struggling upward from the animal stage, either had no family at all or at the most one that does not exist among animals. A being so defenceless as evolving man might well survive in small numbers though living in an isolated state, the highest social form of which is that of pairs such as Westermarck, relying on hunter's reports, attributes to the gorilla and the chimpanzee. Another element is necessary for the elevation out of the animal stage, for the realization of the highest progress found in nature: the replacing of the defencelessness of the single individual by the united strength and co-operation of the whole herd. The transition from beast to man out of conditions of the sort under which the anthropoid apes are living to-day would be absolutely unexplainable. These apes rather give the impression of stray sidelines gradually approaching extinction, and at all events in process of decline. This alone is sufficient to reject all parallels between their family forms and those of primeval man. But mutual tolerance of the grown males, freedom from jealousy, was the first condition for the formation of such large and permanent groups, within which alone the transformation from beast to man could be accomplished. And indeed, what do we find to be the most ancient and original form of the family, undeniably traceable by history and even found to-day here and there? The group marriage, that form in which whole groups of men and whole groups of women mutually belong to one another, leaving only small scope for jealousy. And furthermore we find at a later stage the exceptional form of polyandry which still more supersedes all sentiments of jealousy and hence is unknown to animals.

THE FAMILY

But all the forms of the group marriage known to us are accompanied by such peculiarly complicated circumstances that they of necessity point to a preceding simpler form of sexual intercourse and, hence, in the last instance to a period of unrestricted sexual intercourse corresponding to a transition from the animal to man. Therefore the references to animal marriages lead us back to precisely that point, from which they were intended to remove us forever.

What does the term "unrestricted sexual intercourse" mean? Simply, that the restrictions in force now were not observed formerly. We have already seen the barrier of jealousy falling. If anything is certain, it is that jealousy is developed at a comparatively late stage. The same is true of incest. Not only brother and sister were originally man and wife, but also the sexual intercourse between parents and children is permitted to this day among many nations. Bancroft testifies to the truth of this among the Kaviats of the Behring Strait, the Kadiaks of Alaska, the Tinnehs in the interior of British North America; Letourneau compiled reports of the same fact in regard to the Chippeway Indians, the Coocoos in Chile, the Caribeans, the Carens in Indo-China, not to mention the tales of ancient Greeks and Romans about the Parthians, Persians, Scythians, Huns and so forth. Before incest was invented (and it is an invention, a really valuable one indeed), sexual intercourse between parents and children could not be any more repulsive than between other persons belonging to different generations, which takes place even in our day among the most narrow-minded nations without causing any horror. Even old "maids" of more than sixty years sometimes, if they are rich enough, marry young men of about thirty. Eliminating from the primeval forms of the family known to us those conceptions of incest—conceptions totally different from

THE ORIGIN OF THE FAMILY

ours and often enough in direct contradiction with them—we arrive at a form of sexual intercourse that can only be designated as unrestricted. Unrestricted in the sense that the barriers drawn later on by custom did not yet exist. This in no way necessarily implies for practical purposes an injudicious pell-mell intercourse. The separate existence of pairs for a limited time is not out of the question, and even comprises the majority of cases in the group marriage of our days. And if the latest repudiator of such a primeval state, Westermarck, designates as marriage every case, where both sexes remain mated until the birth of the offspring, then this is equivalent to saying that this kind of marriage may well exist during a stage of unrestricted intercourse without contradicting license, i. e., absence of barriers drawn by custom for sexual intercourse. Westermarck bases himself on the opinion that "license includes the suppression of individual affections" so that "prostitution is its most genuine form." To me it rather seems that any understanding of primeval conditions is impossible as long as we look at them through brothel spectacles. We shall return to this point in the group marriage.

According to Morgan, the following forms developed from this primeval state at an apparently early stage:

1. THE CONSANGUINE FAMILY.

The Consanguine Family is the first step toward the family. Here the marriage groups are arranged by generations: all the grand-fathers and grand-mothers within a certain family are mutually husbands and wives; and equally their children, the fathers and mothers, whose children form a third cycle of mutual mates. The children of these again, the great-grand-children of the first cycle, will form a fourth. In this form of the family, then, only ancestors and descendants are excluded from what we would call the

THE FAMILY

rights and duties of marriage. Brothers and sisters, male and female cousins of the first, second and more remote grades, are all mutually brothers and sisters and for this reason mutual husbands and wives. The relation of brother and sister quite naturally includes at this stage the practice of sexual intercourse.*

The typical form of such a family would consist of the offspring of one pair, representing again the descendants of each grade as mutual brothers and sisters and, therefore, mutual husbands and wives. The consanguine family is extinct. Even the crudest nations of history do not furnish any proofs of it. But the Hawaiian system of kinship, in force to this day in

---

*Author's note. In the spring of 1882, Marx expressed himself in the strongest terms on the total misrepresentation of primeval times by Wagner's Nibelungen text: "Who ever primeval times by Wagner's Nibelungen text: "Whoever heard of a brother embracing his sister as a bride?" To these lascivious Wagnerian gods who in truly modern style are rendering their love quarrels more spicy by a little incest, Marx replies: "In primeval times the sister was the wife and that was moral. (To the fourth edition.) A French friend and admirer of Wagner does not consent to this foot note, and remarks that even in the Oegisdrecka, the more ancient Edda on which Wagner built, Loki denounces Freya: "Before the gods you embraced your own brother." This, he says, proves that marriage between brother and sister was interdicted even then. But the Oegisdrecka is the expression of a time when the belief in the old myths was totally shaken; it is a truly Lucian satire on the gods. If Loki as Mephisto denounces Freya in this manner, then it is rather a point against Wagner. Loki also says, a few verses further on, to Niordhr: "With your sister you generated (such) a son" (vidh systur thinni gatzu slikan mog"). Niordhr is not an Asa, but a Vana, and says in the Ynglinga Saga that marriages between brothers and sisters are sanctioned in Vanaland, which is not the case among the Asas. This would indicate that the Vanas are older gods than the Asas. At any rate Niordhr lived on equal terms with the Asas, and the Oegisdrecka is thus rather a proof that at the time of the origin of the Norwegian mythology the marriage of brother and sister was not yet repulsive, at least not to the gods. In trying to excuse Wagner it might be better to quote Goethe instead of the Edda. This poet commits a similar error in his ballad of the god and the bajadere in regard to the religious surrender of women and approaches modern prostitution far too closely.

THE ORIGIN OF THE FAMILY

all Polynesia, compels us to acknowledge its former existence, for it exhibits grades of kinship that could only originate in this form of the family. And the whole subsequent development of the family compels us to admit this form as a necessary step.

2. THE PUNALUAN FAMILY.

While the first step of organization consisted in excluding parents and children from mutual sexual intercourse, the second was the erection of a barrier between brother and sister. This progress was much more important on account of the greater equality in the ages of the parties concerned, but also far more difficult. It was accomplished gradually, probably beginning with the exclusion of the natural sister (i. e., on the mother's side) from sexual intercourse, first in single cases, then becoming more and more the rule (in Hawaii exceptions were still noted during the nineteenth century); and finally ending with the prohibition of marriage even among collateral brothers and sisters, i. e., what we now term brother's and sister's children, grandchildren, and great-grandchildren. This progress offers, according to Morgan, an excellent illustration how the principle of natural selection works. Without question, the tribes limiting inbreeding by this progress developed faster and more completely than those retaining the marriage between brothers and sisters as a rule and law. And how powerfully the influence of this progress was felt, is shown by the institution of the gens, directly attributable to it and passing far beyond the goal. The gens is the foundation of the social order of most, if not all, barbarian nations, and in Greece and Rome we step immediately from it to civilization.

Every primeval family necessarily had to divide after a few generations. The originally communistic

THE FAMILY

and collective household existing far into the middle stage of barbarism, involved a certain maximum size of the family, variable according to conditions, but still limited in a degree. As soon as the conception of the impropriety of sexual intercourse between children of the same mother arose, it naturally became effective on such occasions as the division of old and the foundation of new household communities (which, however, did not necessarily coincide with the family group). One or more series of sisters became the center of one group, their natural brothers that of another. In this or a similar manner that form which Morgan styles the Punaluan family developed from the consanguine family. According to Hawaiian custom, a number of sisters, natural or more remote (i. e., cousins of the first, second and more remote degrees) were the mutual wives of their mutual husbands, their natural brothers excepted. These men now no longer addressed one another as "brother"—which they no longer had to be—but as "Punalua," i. e., intimate companion, associate as it were. Likewise a series of natural or more remote brothers lived in mutual marriage with a number of women, not their natural sisters, and these women referred to each other as "Punalua." This is the classical form of a family, which later admitted of certain variations. Its fundamental characteristic was mutual community of husbands and wives within a given family with the exclusion of the natural brothers (or sisters) first, and of the more remote grades later.

This form of the family, now, furnishes with complete accuracy the degrees of kinship expressed by the American system. The children of the sisters of my mother still are her children; likewise the children of the brothers of my father still his children; and all of them are my brothers and sisters. But the children of the brothers of my mother are now her nephews and nieces, the children of the sisters of my father his nephew and nieces, and they are all my cousins. For while the husbands of the sisters of my mother are still her husbands, and likewise the wives of the brothers of my father still his wives—legally, if not always in fact—the social proscription of sexual intercourse between brothers and sisters has now divided those relatives who were formerly regarded without distinction as brothers and sisters, into two classes. In one category are those who remain (more remote) brothers and sisters as before; in the other the children of the brother on one hand or the sister on the opposite, who can be brothers and sisters no longer. The latter have mutual parents no more, neither father nor mother nor both together. And for this reason the class of nephews and nieces, male and female cousins, here becomes necessary for the first time. Under the former family order this would have been absurd. The American system of kinship, which appears absolutely paradoxical in any family form founded on monogamy, is rationally explained and naturally confirmed in its most minute details by the Punaluan family. Wherever this system of kinship was in force, there the Punaluan family or at least a form akin to it must also have existed.

This family form, the existence of which in Hawaii was actually demonstrated, would have been transmitted probably by all Polynesia, if the pious missionaries, similar to the Spanish monks in America, could have looked upon such anti-Christian relations as being something more than simply a "horror."*

---

*There is no longer any doubt that the traces of unrestricted sexual intercourse, which Bachofen alleges to have found—called "incestuous generation" by him—are traceable to group marriage. If Bachofen considers those Punaluan marriages "lawless," a man of that period would look upon most of our present marriages between near and remote cousins on the father's or mother's side as incestuous, being marriages between consanguineous relatives."—Marx.

THE FAMILY

Cesar's report to the effect that the Britons, who then were in the middle stage of barbarism, "have ten or twelve women in common, mostly brothers with brothers and parents with children," is best explained by group marriage. Barbarian mothers have not ten or twelve sons old enough to keep women in common, but the American system of kinship corresponding to the Punaluan family furnishes many brothers, because all near and remote cousins of a certain man are his brothers. The term "parents with children" may arise from a wrong conception of Cesar, but this system does not absolutely exclude the existence of father and son, mother or daughter in the same group. It does exclude, however, father and daughter or mother and son. This or a similar form of group marriage also furnishes the easiest explanation of the reports of Herodotus and other ancient writers concerning community of women among savage and barbarian nations. This is true, furthermore, of Watson's and Kaye's* tale about the Tikurs of Audh (north of the Ganges): "They live together (i e., sexually) almost indiscriminately in large communities, and though two persons may be considered as being married, still the tie is only nominal."

The institution of the gens seems to have its origin in the majority of cases in the Punaluan family. True, the Australian class system also offers a starting point for it; the Australians have gentes, but not yet a Punaluan family, only a cruder form of group marriage.*

In all forms of the group family it is uncertain who is the father of a child, but certain, who is its mother. Although she calls all the children of the aggregate family her children and has the duties of a mother toward them, still she knows her natural children from

---
*The People of India.
*See translator's note, p. 55.

THE ORIGIN OF THE FAMILY

others. It is also obvious that, as far as group marriage exists, descent can only be traced on the mother's side and, hence, only female lineage be acknowledged. This is actually the case among all savage tribes and those in the lower stage of barbarism. To have discovered this first is the second great merit of Bachofen. He designates this exclusive recognition of descent from the female line and the hereditary relations resulting therefrom in course of time as "maternal law." I retain this term for the sake of brevity, although it is distorted; for at this social stage there is no sign yet of any law in the juridic sense.

If we now take one of the two standard groups of a Punaluan family, namely that of a series of natural and remote sisters (i. e., first, second and more remote descendants of natural sisters), their children and their natural or remote brothers on the mother's side (who according to our supposition are not their husbands), we have exactly that circle of persons who later appear as members of a gens, in the original form of this institution. They all have a common ancestress, by virtue of the descent that makes the different female generations sisters. But the husbands of these sisters cannot be chosen among their brothers any more, can no longer come from the same ancestress, and do not, therefore, belong to the consanguineous group of relatives, the gens of a later time. The children of these same sisters, however, do belong to this group, because descent from the female line alone is conclusive, alone is positive. As soon as the proscription of sexual intercourse between all relatives on the mother's side, even the most remote of them, is an accomplished fact, the above named group has become a gens, i. e., constitutes a definite circle of consanguineous relatives of female lineage who are not permitted to marry one another. Henceforth this circle is more and more fortified by other mutual insti-

THE FAMILY

tutions of a social or religious character and thus distinguished from other gentes of the same tribe. Of this more anon.

Finding, as we do, that the gens not only necessarily, but also as a matter of course, develops from the Punaluan family, it becomes obvious to us to assume as almost practically demonstrated the prior existence of this family form among all those nations where such gentes are traceable, i. e., nearly all barbarian and civilized nations.

When Morgan wrote his book, our knowledge of group marriage was very limited. We knew very little about the group marriages of the Australians organized in classes, and furthermore Morgan had published as early as 1871 the information he had received about the Punaluan family of Hawaii. This family on one hand furnished a complete explanation of the system of kinship in force among the American Indians, which had been the point of departure for all the studies of Morgan. On the other hand it formed a ready means for the deduction of the maternal law gens. And finally it represented a far higher stage of development than the Australian classes.

It is, therefore, easy to understand how Morgan could regard this form as the stage necessarily preceding the pairing family and attribute general extension in former times to it. Since then we have learned of several other forms of the group marriage, and we know that Morgan went too far in this respect. But it was nevertheless his good fortune to encounter in his Punaluan family the highest, the classical, form of group marriage, that form which gave the simplest clue for the transition to a higher stage.

The most essential contribution to our knowledge of the group marriage we owe to the English missionary, Lorimer Fison, who studied this form of the family for years on its classical ground, Australia. He found

THE ORIGIN OF THE FAMILY

the lowest stage of development among the Papuans near Mount Gambier in South Australia. Here the whole tribe is divided into two great classes, Kroki and Kumite.* Sexual intercourse within each of these classes is strictly prohibited. But every man of one class is by birth the husband of every woman of the other class, and vice versa. Not the individuals are married to one another, but the whole groups, class to class. And mark well, no caution is made anywhere on account of difference of age or special consanguinity, unless it is resulting from the division into two exogamous classes. A Kroki has for his wife every Kumite woman. And as his own daughter, being the daughter of a Kumite woman, is also Kumite according to maternal law, she is therefore the born wife of every Kroki, including her father. At least, the class organization, as we know it, does not exclude this possibility. Hence this organization either arose at a time when, in spite of all dim endeavor to limit inbreeding, sexual intercourse between parents and children was not yet regarded with any particular horror; in this case the class system would be directly evolved from a condition of unrestricted sexual relations. Or the intercourse between parents and children was already proscribed by custom, when the classes were formed; and in this case the present condition points back to the consanguine family and is the first step out of it. The latter case is the more probable. So far as I know, no mention is made of any sexual intercourse between parents and children in Australia. Even the later form of exogamy, the maternal law gens, as a rule silently presupposes that the

---

Translator's note.
*According to Cunow, Kroki and Kumite are phratries. See "Die Verwandschaftsorganizationen der Australneger," by Heinrich Cunow. Stuttgart, Dietz 'Verlag, 1894.

THE FAMILY

prohibition of this intercourse was an accomplished fact at the time of its institution.

The system of two classes is not only found near Mount Gambier in South Australia, but also farther east along Darling River, and in the northeast of Queensland. It is, consequently, widespread. It excludes only marriage between brothers and sisters, between brothers' children and between sisters' children of the mother's side, because these belong to the same class; but the children of a sister can marry those of a brother and vice versa. A further step for preventing inbreeding is found among the Kamilaroi on the Darling River in New South Wales, where the two original classes are split into four, and every one of these is married as a whole to a certain other class. The first two classes are husbands and wives by birth. According to the place of the mother in the first or second class, the children belong to the third and fourth. The children of these two classes, who are also married to one another, again belong to the first and second class. So that a certain generation belongs to the first and second class, the next to the third and fourth and the following again to the first and second. Hence the children of natural brothers and sisters (on the mother's side) cannot marry one another, but their grandchildren can do so. This peculiarly complicated order of things is still more entangled by the inoculation—evidently at a later stage—with maternal law gentes. But we cannot discuss this further. Enough, the desire to prevent inbreeding again and again demands recognition, but feeling its way quite spontaneously, without a clear conception of the goal.

The group marriage is represented in Australia by class marriage, i. e., mass marriage of a whole class of men frequently scattered over the whole breadth of the continent to an equally widespread class of

THE ORIGIN OF THE FAMILY

women. A close view of this group marriage does not offer quite such a horrible spectacle as the philistine imagination accustomed to brothel conditions generally pictures to itself. On the contrary, long years passed, before its existence was even suspected, and quite recently it is once more denied. To the casual observer it makes the impression of a loose monogamy and in certain places of polygamy, with occasional breach of faith. Years are required before one can discover, like Fison and Howitt, the law regulating these marital conditions that rather appeal in their practicability to the average European; the law enabling the strange Papuan, thousands of miles from his home and among people whose language he does not understand, to find frequently, from camp to camp and from tribe to tribe, women who will without resistance and guilelessly surrender to him; the law according to which a man with several women offers one to his guest for the night. Where the European sees immorality and lawlessness, there in reality a strict law is observed. The women belong to the marriage class of the stranger and, therefore, they are his wives by birth. The same moral law assigning both to one another forbids under penalty of proscription all sexual intercourse outside of the two marriage classes. Even when women are abducted, as is frequently the case in certain regions, the class law is carefully respected.

In the abduction of women, by the way, a trace of transition to monogamy is found even here, at least in the form of the pairing family. If a young man has abducted a girl with the help of his friends, they hold sexual intercourse with her one after another. But after that the girl is regarded as the wife of the young man who planned the abduction. And again, if an abducted woman deserts her husband and is caught by another man, she becomes the wife of the

THE FAMILY

latter and the first has lost his privilege. Alongside of and within the generally existing group marriage such exclusive relations are formed, pairing for a shorter or longer term by the side of polygamy, so that here also group marriage is declining. The question is only which will first disappear under the pressure of European influence: group marriage or the Papuans addicted to it.

The marriage in whole classes, such as is in force in Australia, is no doubt a very low and primitive form of group marriage, while the Punaluan family, so far as we know, is its highest stage of delevopment. The former seems to be corresponding to the social stage of roving savages, the latter requires relatively settled communistic bodies and leads directly to the next higher stage of development. Between these two, we shall no doubt find many an intermediate stage. Here lies a barely opened, hardly entered field of investigation.*

Translator's note.

*Heinrich Cunow has given us the results of his most recent investigations in his "Verwandschaftsorganisationen der Australneger." He sums up his studies in these words: "While Morgan and Fison regard the system of marriage classes as an original organization preceding the so-called Punaluan family, I have found that the class is indeed older than the gens, having its origin in the different strata of generations characteristic of the "consanguine family" of Morgan; but the present mode of classification in force among Kamilaroi, Kabi, Yuipera, etc., cannot have arisen until a much later time, when the gentile institution had already grown out of the horde. This system of classification does not represent the first timid steps of evolution; it is not the most primitive of any known forms of social organization, but an intermediate form that takes shape together with the gentile society, a stage of transition to a pure gentile organization. In this stage, the generic classification in strata of different ages belonging to the so-called consanguine family runs parallel for a while with the gentile order. . . . .
It would have been easy for me to quote the testimony of travelers and ethnologists in support of the conclusions drawn by me from the forms of relationship among Australian negroes. But I purposely refrain from doing this,

THE ORIGIN OF THE FAMILY

3. THE PAIRING FAMILY.

A certain pairing for a longer or shorter term took place even during the group marriage or still earlier. A man had his principal wife (one can hardly call it favorite wife as yet) among many women, and he was to her the principal husband among others. This fact in no small degree contributed to the confusion among missionaries, who regarded group marriage now as a disorderly community of women, now as an arbitrary adultery. Such a habitual pairing would gain ground the more the gens developed and the more numerous the classes of "brothers" and "sisters" became who were not permitted to marry one another. The impulse to prevent marriage of consanguineous relatives started by the gens went still further. Thus we find that among the Iroquois and

---

with a few exceptions, first because I do not wish to write a general history of the primitive family, and, secondly, because I consider all references of this kind as very doubtful testimony, unless they are accompanied by an analysis of the entire organization. We frequently find analogies to the institutions of a lower stage in a high stage, and yet they are founded on radically different premises and causes. The evolution of the Australian aborigines shows that. Among the Australians of the lower stage, e. g., the hordes are endogamous, among those of the middle stage they are exogamous, and in the higher stage they are again endogamous. But while in the one instance the marriage in the horde is conditioned on the fact that the more remote relatives are not yet excluded from sexual intercourse, it is founded in the other case on the difference between local and sexual organization. Furthermore, the marriage between daughter and father is permitted in the lower stage, and again in that higher stage, where the class organization of the Kamilaroi is on the verge of dissolution. But in both cases the circle of those who are regarded as fathers is entirely different. The character of an institution can only be perfectly understood, if we examine its connection with the entire organization, and, if possible, trace its metamorphoses in the preceding stages. . . . .

The characteristic feature of the class system is that by the side of the gentile order, such as is found among the North American Indians, there is always another system of four marriage classes for the purpose of limiting sexual intercourse between certain groups of relatives. Neither the phratry nor the gens of the Kamilaroi forms a distinct terri-

THE FAMILY

most of the Indians in the lower stage of barbarism marriage is prohibited between all the relatives of their system of kinship, and this comprises several hundred kinds. By this increasing complication of marriage restrictions, group marriage became more and more impossible; it was displaced by the pairing family. At this stage one man lives with one woman, but in such a manner that polygamy, and occasional adultery, remain privileges of men, although the former occurs rarely for economic reasons. Women, however, are generally expected to be strictly faithful during the time of living together, and adultery on their part is cruelly punished. But the marriage-tie may be easily broken by either party, and the children belong to the mother alone, as formerly.

---

torial community. Their members are scattered among different roving hordes, and they only meet occasionally, e. g., to celebrate a feast or dance. . . . . .

The origin of gentile systems out of Punaluan groups has never been proven, while we see among the Australian negroes that the classes are clearly and irrefutably in existence among the first traces of gentilism. . . . . .

The class system in its original form is a conclusive proof of Morgan's theory, that the first step in the formation of systems of relationship consisted in prohibiting sexual intercourse between parents and children (in a wider sense). . . . . .

It has been often disputed that the Punaluan family ever existed outside of the Sandwich Islands. But the marriage institutions of certain Australian tribes named by me prove the contrary. The Pirrauru of the Dieyerie is absolutely identical with the Punalua of the Hawaiians; and these institutions were not described by travelers who rushed through the territories of those tribes without knowing their language, but by men who lived among them for decades and fully mastered their dialects. . . . . .

I have shown how far the class system corresponds to the Hawaiian system. It is and remains a fact, that it contains a long series of terms that cannot be explained by the relations in the so-called consanguine family, and the use of which creates confusion, if applied to this family. But that simply shows that Morgan was mistaken about the age and present structure of the Hawaiian system. It does not prove that it could not have grown on the basis assumed by him. . . . . .

If the opponents of Morgan dispute that the so-called con-

THE ORIGIN OF THE FAMILY

In this ever more extending restriction of marriage between consanguineous relations, natural selection also remains effective. As Morgan expresses it: "Marriages between gentes that were not consanguineous produced a more vigorous race, physically and mentally; two progressive tribes intermarried, and the new skulls and brains naturally expanded until they comprised the faculties of both." Thus tribes composed of gentes necessarily either gained the supremacy over the backward ones or, by their example, carried them along in their wake.

The development of the family, then, is founded on the continual contraction of the circle, originally comprising the whole tribe, within which marital intercourse between both sexes was general. By the con-

---

sanguine family is based on blood kinship, they are right, unless we wish to assign an exceptional position to the Australian strata of generations. But if they go further and declare that the subsequent restrictions of inbreeding and the gentile order have arisen independently of relationships, they commit a far greater mistake than Morgan. They block their way to an understanding of subsequent organizations and force themselves to all sorts of queer assumptions that at once appear as the fruits of imagination, when compared with the actual institutions of primitive peoples. . . . . .

This explanation of the phases of development of family institutions contradicts present day views on the matter. Since the scientific investigations of the last decade have demonstrated beyond doubt that the so-called patriarchal family was preceded by the matriarchal family, it has become the custom to regard descent by females as a natural institution belonging to the very first stages of development which is explained by the modes of existence and thought among savages. Paternity being a matter of speculation, maternity of actual observation, it is supposed to follow that descent by females was always recognized. But the development of the Australian systems of relationship shows that this is not true, at least not in regard to Australians. The fact cannot be disputed away, that we find female lineage among all those higher developed tribes that have progressed to the formation of gentile organizations, but male lineage among all those that have no gentile organizations or where these are only in process of formation. Not a single tribe has been discovered so far, where female lineage was not combined with gentile organization, and I doubt that any will ever be found.

THE FAMILY

tinual exclusion, first of near, then of ever remoter relatives, including finally even those who were simply related legally, all group marriage becomes practically impossible. At last only one couple, temporarily and loosely united, remains; that molecule, the dissolution of which absolutely puts an end to marriage. Even from this we may infer how little the sexual love of the individual in the modern sense of the word had to do with the origin of monogamy. The practice of all nations of that stage still more proves this. While in the previous form of the family the men were never embarrassed for women, but rather had more than enough of them, women now became scarce and were sought after. With the pairing family, therefore, the abduction and barter of women began—widespread symptoms, and nothing but that, of a new and much more profound change. The pedantic Scot, McLennan, however, transmuted these symptoms, mere methods of obtaining women, into separate classes of the family under the head of "marriage by capture" and "marriage by barter." Moreover among American Indians and other nations in the same stage, the marriage agreement is not the business of the parties most concerned, who often are not even asked, but of their mothers. Frequently two persons entirely unknown to one another are thus engaged to be married and receive no information of the closing of the bargain, until the time for the marriage ceremony approaches. Before the wedding, the bridegroom brings gifts to the maternal relatives of the bride (not to her father or his relatives) as an equivalent for ceding the girl to him. Either of the married parties may dissolve the marriage at will. But among many tribes, as, e. g., the Iroquois, public opinion has gradually become averse to such separations. In case of domestic differences the gentile relatives of both parties endeavor to bring about a reconciliation, and not until

THE ORIGIN OF THE FAMILY

they are unsuccessful a separation takes place. In this case the woman keeps the children, and both parties are free to marry again.

The pairing family, being too weak and too unstable to make an independent household necessary or even desirable, in no way dissolves the traditional communistic way of housekeeping. But household communism implies supremacy of women in the house as surely as exclusive recognition of a natural mother and the consequent impossibility of identifying the natural father signify high esteem for women, i. e., mothers. It is one of the most absurd notions derived from eighteenth century enlightenment, that in the beginning of society woman was the slave of man. Among all savages and barbarians of the lower and middle stages, sometimes even of the higher stage, women not only have freedom, but are held in high esteem. What they were even in the pairing family, let Arthur Wright, for many years a missionary among the Seneca Iroquois, testify: "As to their families, at a time when they still lived in their old long houses (communistic households of several families) . . . a certain clan (gens) always reigned, so that the women choose their husbands from other clans (gentes). . . . The female part generally ruled the house; the provisions were held in common; but woe to the luckless husband or lover who was too indolent or too clumsy to contribute his share to the common stock. No matter how many children or how much private property he had in the house, he was liable at any moment to receive a hint to gather up his belongings and get out. And he could not dare to venture any resistance; the house was made too hot for him and he had no other choice, but to return to his own clan (gens) or, as was mostly the case, to look for another wife in some other clan. The women were the dominating power in the clans (gentes) and

THE FAMILY

everywhere else. Occasionally they did not hesitate to dethrone a chief and degrade him to a common warrior."

The communistic household, in which most or all the women belong to one and the same gens, while the husbands come from different gentes, is the cause and foundation of the general and widespread supremacy of women in primeval times. The discovery of this fact is the third merit of Bachofen.

By way of supplement I wish to state that the reports of travelers and missionaries concerning the overburdening of women among savages and barbarians do not in the least contradict the above statements. The division of labor between both sexes is caused by other reasons than the social condition of women. Nations, where women have to work much harder than is proper for them in our opinion, often respect women more highly than Europeans do. The lady of civilized countries, surrounded with sham homage and a stranger to all real work stands on a far lower social level than a hard-working barbarian woman, regarded as a real lady (frowa-lady-mistress) and having the character of such.

Whether or not the pairing family has in our time entirely supplanted group marriage in America, can be decided only by closer investigations among those nations of northwestern and especially of southern America that are still in the higher stage of savagery. About the latter so many reports of sexual license are current that the assumption of a complete cessation of the ancient group marriage is hardly warranted. Evidently all traces of it have not yet disappeared. In at least forty North American tribes the man marrying an elder sister has the right to make all her sisters his wives as soon as they are of age, a survival of the community of men for the whole series of sisters. And Bancroft relates that the Indians of

THE ORIGIN OF THE FAMILY

the Californian peninsula celebrate certain festivities uniting several "tribes" for the purpose of unrestricted sexual intercourse. These are evidently gentes that have preserved in these festivities a vague recollection of the time when the women of one gens had for their common husbands all the men of another gens, and vice versa. The same custom is still observed in Australia. Among certain nations it sometimes happens that the older men, the chief and sorcerer-priests, exploit the community of women for their own benefits and monopolize all the women. But in their turn they must restore the old community during certain festivities and great assemblies, permitting their wives to enjoy themselves with the young men. A whole series of examples of such periodical saturnalia restoring for a short time the ancient sexual freedom is quoted by Westermarck:* among the Hos, the Santals, the Punjas and Kotars in India, among some African nations, etc. Curiously enough Westermarck concludes that this is a survival, not of group marriage, the existence of which he denies, but—of a rutting season which primitive man had in common with other animals.

Here we touch Bachofen's fourth great discovery: the widespread form of transition from group marriage to pairing family. What Bachofen represents as a penance for violating the old divine laws—the penalty with which a woman redeems her right to chastity, is in fact only a mystical expression for the penalty paid by a woman for becoming exempt from the ancient community of men and acquiring the right of surrendering to one man only. This penalty consists in a limited surrender: Babylonian women had to surrender once a year in the temple of Mylitta; other nations of Western Asia sent their young women

*The History of Human Marriage, p. 28-29.

THE FAMILY

for years to the temple of Anaitis, where they had to practice free love with favorites of their own choice before they were allowed to marry. Similar customs in a religious disguise are common to nearly all Asiatic nations between the Mediterranean and the Ganges. The penalty for exemption becomes gradually lighter in course of time, as Bachofen remarks: "The annually repeated surrender gives place to a single sacrifice; the hetaerism of the matrons is followed by that of the maidens, the promiscuous intercourse during marriage to that before wedding, the indiscriminate intercourse with all to that with certain individuals."* Among some nations the religious disguise is missing. Among others—Thracians, Celts, etc., in classic times, many primitive inhabitants of India, Malay nations, South Sea Islanders and many American Indians to this day—the girls enjoy absolute sexual freedom before marriage. This is especially true almost everywhere in South America, as everybody can confirm who penetrates a little into the interior. Agassiz, e. g., relates* an anecdote of a wealthy family of Indian descent. On being introduced to the daughter he asked something about her father, presuming him to be her mother's husband, who was in the war against Paraguay. But the mother replied, smiling: "Nao tem pai, he filha da fortuna"—she hasn't any father; she is the daughter of chance. "It is the way the Indian or half-breed women here always speak of their illegitimate children; and though they say it without an intonation of sadness or of blame, apparently as unconscious of any wrong or shame as if they said the father was absent or dead, it has the most melancholy significance; it seems to speak of such absolute desertion. So far is this from being an

---

*Mutterrecht, p. xix.
*A Journey in Brazil. Boston and New York, 1886. Page 266.

THE ORIGIN OF THE FAMILY

unusual case, that among the common people the opposite seems the exception. Children are frequently quite ignorant of their parentage. They know about their mother, for all the care and responsibility falls upon her, but they have no knowledge of their father; nor does it seem to occur to the woman that she or her children have any claim upon him." What seems so strange to the civilized man, is simply the rule of maternal law and group marriage.

Again, among other nations the friends and relatives of the bridegroom or the wedding guests claim their traditional right to the bride, and the bridegroom comes last. This custom prevailed in ancient times on the Baleares and among the African Augilers; it is observed to this day by the Bareas in Abyssinia. In still other cases, an official person—the chief of a tribe or a gens, the cazique, shamane, priest, prince or whatever may be his title—represents the community and exercises the right of the first night. All modern romantic whitewashing notwithstanding, this jus primae noctis, is still in force among most of the natives of Alaska,* among the Tahus of northern Mexico** and some other nations. And during the whole of the middle ages it was practised at least in originally Celtic countries, where it was directly transmitted by group marriage, e. g. in Aragonia. While in Castilia the peasant was never a serf, the most disgraceful serfdom existed in Aragonia, until abolished by the decision of Ferdinand the Catholic in 1486. In this document we read: "We decide and declare that the aforesaid 'senyors' (barons) . . . . . shall neither sleep the first night with the wife of a peasant, nor shall they in the first night after the wedding, when the woman has gone to bed, step over said woman or

---
*Bancroft, Native Races, I., 81.
**Ibidem, p. 584.

THE FAMILY

bed as a sign of their authority. Neither shall the aforesaid senyors use the daughter or the son of any peasant, with or without pay, against their will." (Quoted in the Catalonian original by Sugenheim, "Serfdom," Petersburg, 1861, page 35.)

Bachofen, furthermore, is perfectly right in contending that the transition from what he calls "hetaerism" or "incestuous generation" to monogamy was brought about mainly by women. The more in the course of economic development, undermining the old communism and increasing the density of population, the traditional sexual relations lost their innocent character suited to the primitive forest, the more debasing and oppressive they naturally appeared to women; and the more they consequently longed for relief by the right of chastity, of temporary or permanent marriage with one man. This progress could not be due to men for the simple reason that they never, even to this day, had the least intention of renouncing the pleasures of actual group marriage. Not until the women had accomplished the transition to the pairing family could the men introduce strict monogamy—true, only for women.

The pairing family arose on the boundary line between savagery and barbarism, generally in the higher stage of savagery, here and there in the lower stage of barbarism. It is the form of the family characteristic for barbarism, as group marriage is for savagery and monogamy for civilization. In order to develop it into established monogamy, other causes than those active hitherto were required. In the pairing family the group was already reduced to its last unit, its biatomic molecule: one man and one woman. Natural selection had accomplished its purpose by a continually increasing restriction of sexual intercourse. Nothing remained to be done in this direction. Unless new social forces became active, there was no reason why

THE ORIGIN OF THE FAMILY

a new form of the family should develop out of the pairing family. But these forces did become active.

We now leave America, the classic soil of the pairing family. No sign permits the conclusion that a higher form of the family was developed here, that any established form of monogamy ever existed anywhere in the New World before the discovery and conquest. Not so in the Old World.

In the latter, the domestication of animals and the breeding of flocks had developed a hitherto unknown source of wealth and created entirely new social conditions. Up to the lower stage of barbarism, fixed wealth was almost exclusively represented by houses, clothing, rough ornaments and the tools for obtaining and preparing food: boats, weapons and household articles of the simplest kind. Nourishment had to be secured afresh day by day. But now, with their herds of horses, camels, donkeys, cattle, sheep, goats and hogs, the advancing nomadic nations—the Aryans in the Indian Punjab, in the region of the Ganges and the steppes of the Oxus and Jaxartes, then still more rich in water-veins than now; the Semites on the Euphrates and Tigris—had acquired possessions demanding only the most crude attention and care in order to propagate themselves in ever increasing numbers and yield the most abundant store of milk and meat. All former means of obtaining food were now forced to the background. Hunting, once a necessity, now became a sport.

But who was the owner of this new wealth? Doubtless it was originally the gens. However, private ownership of flocks must have had an early beginning. It is difficult to say whether to the author of the so-called first book of Moses Father Abraham appeared as the owner of his flocks by virtue of his privilege as head of a communistic family or of his capacity as gentile chief by actual descent. So much is certain:

THE FAMILY

we must not regard him as a proprietor in the modern sense of the word. It is furthermore certain that everywhere on the threshold of documentary history we find the flocks in the separate possession of chiefs of families, exactly like the productions of barbarian art, such as metal ware, articles of luxury and, finally, the human cattle—the slaves.

For now slavery was also invented. To the barbarian of the lower stage a slave was of no use. The American Indians, therefore, treated their vanquished enemies in quite a different way from nations of a higher stage. The men were tortured or adopted as brothers into the tribe of the victors. The women were married or likewise adopted with their surviving children. The human labor power at this stage does not yet produce a considerable amount over and above its cost of subsistence. But the introduction of cattle raising, metal industry, weaving and finally agriculture wrought a change. Just as the once easily obtainable wives now had an exchange value and were bought, so labor power was now procured, especially since the flocks had definitely become private property. The family did not increase as rapidly as the cattle. More people were needed for superintending; for this purpose the captured enemy was available and, besides, he could be increased by breeding like the cattle.

Such riches, once they had become the private property of certain families and augmented rapidly, gave a powerful impulse to society founded on the pairing family and the maternal gens. The pairing family had introduced a new element. By the side of the natural mother it had placed the authentic natural father who probably was better authenticated than many a "father" of our day. According to the division of labor in those times, the task of obtaining food and the tools necessary for this purpose fell to

THE ORIGIN OF THE FAMILY

the share of the man; hence he owned the latter and kept them in case of a separation, as the women did the household goods. According to the social custom of that time, the man was also the owner of the new source of existence, the cattle, and later on of the new labor power, the slaves. But according to the same custom, his children could not inherit his property, for the following reasons: By maternal law, i. e., while descent was traced only along the female line, and by the original custom of inheriting in the gens, the gentile relatives inherited the property of their deceased gentile relative. The wealth had to remain in the gens. In view of the insignificance of the objects, the property may have gone in practice to the closest gentile relatives, i. e., the consanguine relatives on the mother's side. The children of the dead man, however, did not belong to his gens, but to that of their mother. They inherited first together with the other consanguine relatives of the mother, later on perhaps in preference to the others. But they could not inherit from their father, because they did not belong to his gens, where his property had to remain. Hence, after the death of a cattle owner, the cattle would fall to his brothers, sisters and the children of his sisters, or to the offspring of the sisters of his mother. His own children were disinherited.

In the measure of the increasing wealth man's position in the family became superior to that of woman, and the desire arose to use this fortified position for the purpose of overthrowing the traditional law of inheritance in favor of his children. But this was not feasible as long as maternal law was valid. This law had to be abolished, and it was. This was by no means as difficult as it appears to us to-day. For this revolution—one of the most radical ever experienced by humanity—did not have to touch a single living member of the gens. All its members could remain

THE FAMILY

what they had always been. The simple resolution was sufficient, that henceforth the offspring of the male members should belong to the gens, while the children of the female members should be excluded by transferring them to the gens of their father. This abolished the tracing of descent by female lineage and the maternal right of inheritance, and instituted descent by male lineage and the paternal right of inheritance. How and when this revolution was accomplished by the nations of the earth, we do not know. It belongs entirely to prehistoric times. That it was accomplished is proven more than satisfactorily by the copious traces of maternal law collected especially by Bachofen. How easily it is accomplished we may observe in a whole series of Indian tribes, that recently passed through or are still engaged in it, partly under the influence of increasing wealth and changed modes of living (transfer from forests to the prairie), partly through the moral pressure of civilization and missionaries. Six out of eight Missouri tribes have male descent and inheritance, while only two retain female descent and inheritance. The Shawnees, Miamis and Delawares follow the custom of placing their children into the male gens by giving them a gentile name belonging to the father's gens, so that they may be entitled to inherit. "Innate casuistry of man, to change the objects by changing their names, and to find loopholes for breaking tradition inside of tradition where a direct interest was a sufficient motive." (Marx.) This made confusion worse confounded, which could be and partially was remedied alone by paternal law. "This seems to be the most natural transition." (Marx.) As to the opinion of the comparative jurists, how this transition took place among the civilized nations of the old world—although only in hypotheses—compare M. Kovalevsky, Tableau

THE ORIGIN OF THE FAMILY

des origines et de l'évolution de la famille et de la propriété, Stockholm, 1890.

The downfall of maternal law was the historic defeat of the female sex. The men seized the reins also in the house, the women were stripped of their dignity, enslaved, tools of men's lust and mere machines for the generation of children. This degrading position of women, especially conspicuous among the Greeks of heroic and still more of classic times, was gradually glossed over and disguised or even clad in a milder form. But it is by no means obliterated.

The first effect of the established supremacy of men became now visible in the reappearance of the intermediate form of the patriarchal family. Its most significant feature is not polygamy, of which more anon, but "the organization of a certain number of free and unfree persons into one family under the paternal authority of the head of the family. In the Semitic form this head of the family lives in polygamy, the unfree members have wife and children, and the purpose of the whole organization is the tending of herds in a limited territory." The essential points are the assimilation of the unfree element and the paternal authority. Hence the ideal type of this form of the family is the Roman family. The word familia did not originally signify the composite ideal of sentimentality and domestic strife in the present day philistine mind. Among the Romans it did not even apply in the beginning to the leading couple and its children, but to the slaves alone. Famulus means domestic slave, and familia is the aggregate number of slaves belonging to one man. At the time of Gajus, the familia, id est patrimonium (i. e., paternal legacy), was still bequeathed by testament. The expression was invented by the Romans in order to designate a new social organism, the head of which had a wife, children and a number of slaves under his paternal

THE FAMILY

authority and according to Roman law the right of life and death over all of them. "The word is, therefore, not older than the ironclad family system of the Latin tribes, which arose after the introduction of agriculture and of lawful slavery, and after the separation of the Aryan Itali from the Greeks." Marx adds: "The modern family contains the germ not only of slavery (servitus), but also of serfdom, because it has from the start a relation to agricultural service. It comprises in miniature all those contrasts that later on develop more broadly in society and the state."

Such a form of the family shows the transition from the pairing family to monogamy. In order to secure the faithfulness of the wife, and hence the reliability of paternal lineage, the women are delivered absolutely into the power of the men; in killing his wife, the husband simply exercises his right.

With the patriarchal family we enter the domain of written history, a field in which comparative law can render considerable assistance. And here it has brought about considerable progress indeed. We owe to Maxim Kovalevsky (Tableau etc. de la famille et de la propriété, Stockholm, 1890, p. 60-100) the proof, that the patriarchal household community, found to this day among Serbians and Bulgarians under the names of Zádruga (friendly bond) and Bratstvo (fraternity), and in a modified form among oriental nations, formed the stage of transition between the maternal family derived from group marriage and the monogamous family of the modern world. This seems at least established for the historic nations of the old world, for Aryans and Semites.

The Zádruga of southern Slavonia offers the best still existing illustration of such a family communism. It comprises several generations of the father's descendants, together with their wives, all living to-

THE ORIGIN OF THE FAMILY

gether on the same farm, tilling their fields in common, living and clothing themselves from the same stock, and possessing collectively the surplus of their earnings. The community is managed by the master of the house (domácin), who acts as its representative, may sell inferior objects, has charge of the treasury and is responsible for it as well as for a proper business administration. He is chosen by vote and is not necessarily the oldest man. The women and their work are directed by the mistress of the house (domácica), who is generally the wife of the domácin. She also has an important, and often final, voice in choosing a husband for the girls. But the highest authority is vested in the family council, the assembly of all grown companions, male and female. The domácin is responsible to this council. It takes all important resolutions, sits in judgment on the members of the household, decides the question of important purchases and sales, especially of land, etc. .

It is only about ten years since the existence of such family communism in the Russia of to-day was proven. At present it is generally acknowledged to be rooted in popular Russian custom quite as much as the obscina or village community.

It is found in the oldest Russian code, the Pravda of Jaroslav, under the same name (vervj) as in the Dalmatian code, and may also be traced in Polish and Czech historical records.

Likewise among Germans, the economic unit according to Heussler (Institutions of German law) is not originally the single family, but the "collective household," comprising several generations or single families and, besides, often enough unfree individuals. The Roman family is also traced to this type, and hence the absolute authority of the master of the house and the defenselessness of the other members in regard to him is strongly questioned of late. Simi-

THE FAMILY

lar communities are furthermore said to have existed among the Celts of Ireland. In France they were preserved up to the time of the Revolution in Nivernais under the name of "parçonneries," and in the Franche Comté they are not quite extinct yet. In the region of Louhans (Saône et Loire) we find large farmhouses with a high central hall for common use reaching up to the roof and surrounded by sleeping rooms accessible by the help of stairs with six to eight steps. Several generations of the same family live together in such a house.

In India, the household community with collective agriculture is already mentioned by Nearchus at the time of Alexander the Great, and it exists to this day in the same region, in the Punjab and the whole Northwest of the country. In the Caucasus it was located by Kovalevski himself.

In Algeria it is still found among the Kabyles. Even in America it is said to have existed. It is supposed to be identical with the "Calpullis" described by Zurita in ancient Mexico. In Peru, however, Cunow (Ausland, 1890, No. 42-44) has demonstrated rather clearly that at the time of the conquest a sort of a constitution in marks (called curiously enough marca), with a periodical allotment of arable soil, and consequently individual tillage, was in existence.

At any rate, the patriarchal household community with collective tillage and ownership of land now assumes an entirely different meaning than heretofore. We can no longer doubt that it played an important role among the civilized and some other nations of the old world in the transition from the maternal to the single family. Later on we shall return to Kovalesky's further conclusion that it was also the stage of transition from which developed the village or mark community with individual tillage and first periodical, then permanent allotment of arable and pasture lands.

THE ORIGIN OF THE FAMILY

In regard to the family life within these household communities it must be remarked that at least in Russia the master of the house has the reputation of strongly abusing his position against the younger women of the community, especially his daughters-in-law, and of transforming them into a harem for himself. Russian popular songs are very eloquent on this point.

Before taking up monogamy, which rapidly developed after the downfall of maternal law, let me say a few words about polygamy and polyandry. Both forms of the family can only be exceptions, historical products of luxury so to speak, unless they could be found side by side in the same country, which is apparently not the case. As the men excluded from polygamy cannot find consolation in the women left over by polyandry, the number of men and women being hitherto approximately equal without regard to social institutions, it becomes of itself impossible to confer on any one of these two forms the distinction of general preference. Indeed, the polygamy of one man was evidently the product of slavery, confined to certain exceptional positions. In the Semitic patriarchal family, only the patriarch himself, or at best a few of his sons, practice polygamy, the others must be satisfied with one wife. This is the case to-day in the whole Orient. Polygamy is a privilege of the wealthy and distinguished, and is mainly realized by purchase of female slaves. The mass of the people live in monogamy. Polyandry in India and Thibet is likewise an exception. Its surely not uninteresting origin from group marriage requires still closer investigation. In its practice it seems, by the way, much more tolerant than the jealous Harem establishment of the Mohammedans. At least among the Nairs of India, three, four or more men have indeed one woman in common; but every one of them may

THE FAMILY

have a second woman in common with three or more other men; and in the same way a third, fourth, etc. It is strange that McLennan did not discover the new class of "club marriage" in these marital clubs, in several of which one may be a member and which he himself describes. This marriage club business is, however, by no means actual polyandry. It is on the contrary, as Giraud-Teulon already remarks, a specialized form of group marriage. The men live in polygamy, the women in polyandry.

4. THE MONOGAMOUS FAMILY.

It develops from the pairing family, as we have already shown, during the time of transition from the middle to the higher stage of barbarism. Its final victory is one of the signs of beginning civilization. It is founded on male supremacy for the pronounced purpose of breeding children of indisputable paternal lineage. The latter is required, because these children shall later on inherit the fortune of their father. The monogamous family is distinguished from the pairing family by the far greater durability of wedlock, which can no longer be dissolved at the pleasure of either party. As a rule, it is only the man who can still dissolve it and cast off his wife. The privilege of conjugal faithlessness remains sanctioned for men at least by custom (the Code Napoleon concedes it directly to them, as long as they do not bring their concubines into the houses of their wives). This privilege is more and more enjoyed with the increasing development of society. If the woman remembers the ancient sexual practices and attempts to revive them, she is punished more severely than ever.

The whole severity of this new form of the family confronts us among the Greeks. While, as Marx observes, the position of the female gods in mythology shows an earlier period, when women still occupied

THE ORIGIN OF THE FAMILY

a freer and more respected plane, we find woman already degraded by the supremacy of man and the competition of slaves during the time of the heroes. Read in the Odysseia how Telemachos reproves and silences his mother. The captured young women, according to Homer, are delivered to the sensual lust of the victors. The leaders in the order of their rank select the most beautiful captives. The whole Iliad notoriously revolves around the quarrel between Achilles and Agamemnon about such a captured woman. In mentioning any hero of importance, the captured girl sharing his tent and bed is never omitted. These girls are also taken into the hero's home country and his house, as Kassandra by Agamemnon in Aeschylos. Boys born by these female slaves receive a small share of the paternal heirloom and are regarded as free men. Teukros is such an illegitimate son and may use his father's name. The wife is expected to put up with everything, while herself remaining chaste and faithful. Although the Greek woman of heroic times is more highly respected than she of the civilized period, still she is for her husband only the mother of his legal heirs, his first housekeeper and the superintendent of the female slaves, whom he can and does make his concubines at will.

It is this practice of slavery by the side of monogamy, the existence of young and beautiful female slaves belonging without any restriction to their master, which from the very beginning gives to monogamy the specific character of being monogamy for women only, but not for men. And this character remains to this day.

For the Greeks of later times we must make a distinction between Dorians and Ionians. The former, with Sparta as their classic example, have in many respects still more antiquated marriage customs than even Homer illustrates. In Sparta existed a form of

THE FAMILY

the pairing family modified by the contemporaneous ideas of the state and still recalling group marriage in many ways. Sterile marriages were dissolved. King Anaxandridas (about 650 before Christ) took another wife besides his childless one and kept two households. About the same time King Ariston added another wife to two childless ones, one of which he dismissed. Furthermore, several brothers could have one wife in common; a friend who liked his friend's wife better than his own could share her with him, and it was not considered indecent to place a wife at the disposal of a sturdy "stallion," as Bismarck would have said, even though he might not be a citizen. A certain passage in Plutarch, where a Spartan matron refers a lover, who persists in making offers to her, to her husband, seems to indicate—according to Schoemann—even a still greater sexual freedom. Also adultery, faithlessness of a wife behind her husband's back, was unheard of. On the other hand, domestic slavery in Sparta, at least during the best time, was unknown, and the serf Helots lived on separate country seats. Hence there was less temptation for a Spartan to hold intercourse with other women. As was to be expected under such circumstances, the women of Sparta occupied a more highly respected place than those of other Greeks. Spartan women and the Athenian hetaerae were the only Greek women of whom the ancients speak respectfully and whose remarks they considered worthy of notice.

Quite a different condition among Ionians, whose representative is Athens. The girls learned only to spin, weave and sew, at the most a little reading and writing. They were practically shut in and had only the company of other women.

The women's room formed a separate part of the house, on the upper floor or in a rear building, where men, especially strangers, did not easily enter and

THE ORIGIN OF THE FAMILY

whither the women retreated when male visitors came. The women did not leave the house without being accompanied by a female slave. At home they were strictly guarded. Aristophanes speaks of Molossian dogs that were kept to frighten off adulterers. And at least in the Asiatic towns, eunuchs were kept for guarding women. Even at Herodotus' time these eunuchs were manufactured for the trade, and according to Wachsmuth not for barbarians alone. By Euripides woman is designated as "oikurema," a neuter signifying an object for housekeeping, and beside the business of breeding children she served to the Athenian for nothing but his chief house maid. The man had his gymnastic exercises, his public meetings, from which the women were excluded. Besides, the man very often had female slaves at his disposal, and during the most flourishing time of Athens an extensive prostitution which was at least patronized by the state. It was precisely on the basis of this prostitution that the unique type of Ionic women developed; the hetaerae. They rose by esprit and artistic taste as far above the general level of antique womanhood as the Spartan women by their character. But that it was necessary to become a hetaera before one could be a woman, constitutes the severest denunciation of the Athenian family.

The Athenian family became in the course of time the model after which not only the rest of the Ionians, but gradually all the Greeks at home and abroad molded their domestic relations. Nevertheless, in spite of all seclusion and watching, the Grecian ladies found sufficient opportunity for deceiving their husbands. The latter who would have been ashamed of betraying any love for their wives, found recreation in all kinds of love affairs with hetaerae. But the degradation of the women was avenged in the men and degraded them also, until they sank into

THE FAMILY

the abomination of boy-love. They degraded their gods and themselves by the myth of Ganymedes.

Such was the origin of monogamy, as far as we may trace it in the most civilized and most highly developed nation of antiquity. It was by no means a fruit of individual sex-love and had nothing to do with the latter, for the marriages remained as conventional as ever. Monogamy was the first form of the family not founded on natural, but on economic conditions, viz.: the victory of private property over primitive and natural collectivism. Supremacy of the man in the family and generation of children that could be his offspring alone and were destined to be the heirs of his wealth—these were openly avowed by the Greeks to be the sole objects of monogamy. For the rest it was a burden to them, a duty to the gods, the state and their own ancestors, a duty to be fulfilled and no more. In Athens the law enforced not only the marriage, but also the fulfillment of a minimum of the so-called matrimonial duties on the man's part.

Monogamy, then, does by no means enter history as a reconciliation of man and wife and still less as the highest form of marriage. On the contrary, it enters as the subjugation of one sex by the other, as the proclamation of an antagonism between the sexes unknown in all preceding history. In an old unpublished manuscript written by Marx and myself in 1846, I find the following passage: "The first division of labor is that of man and wife in breeding children." And to-day I may add: The first class antagonism appearing in history coincides with the development of the antagonism of man and wife in monogamy, and the first class oppression with that of the female by the male sex. Monogamy was a great historical progress. But by the side of slavery and private property it marks at the same time that epoch which, reaching down to our days, takes with all progress also a step backwards, relatively speaking, and develops the welfare and advancement of one by the woe and submission of the other. It is the cellular form of civilized society which enables us to study the nature of its now fully developed contrasts and contradictions.

The old relative freedom of sexual intercourse by no means disappeared with the victory of the pairing or even of the monogamous family. "The old conjugal system, now reduced to narrower limits by the gradual disappearance of the punaluan groups, still environed the advancing family, which it was to follow to the verge of civilization. . . . It finally disappeared in the new form of hetaerism, which still follows mankind in civilization as a dark shadow upon the family."*

By hetaerism Morgan designates sexual intercourse of men with unmarried women outside of the monogamous family, flourishing, as is well known, during the whole period of civilization in many different forms and tending more and more to open prostitution. This hetaerism is directly derived from group marriage, from the sacrificial surrender of women for the purpose of obtaining the right to chastity. The surrender for money was at first a religious act; it took place in the temple of the goddess of love and the money flowed originally into the treasury of the temple. The hierodulae of Anaitis in Armenia, of Aphrodite in Corinth and the religious dancing girls of India attached to the temples, the so-called bajaderes (derived from the Portuguese "bailadera," dancing girl), were the first prostitutes. The surrender, originally the duty of every woman, was later on practiced by these priestesses alone in rep-

---

*Morgan, Ancient Society, p. 504.

THE FAMILY

resentation of all others. Among other nations, hetaerism is derived from the sexual freedom permitted to girls before marriage—also a survival of the group marriage, only transmitted by another route. With the rise of different property relations, in the higher stage of barbarism, wage labor appears sporadically by the side of slavery, and at the same time its unavoidable companion, professional prostitution of free women by the side of the forced surrender of female slaves. It is the heirloom bequeathed by group marriage to civilization, a gift as ambiguous as everything else produced by ambiguous, double-faced, schismatic and contradictory civilization. Here monogamy, there hetaerism and its most extreme form, prostitution. Hetaerism is as much a social institution as all others. It continues the old sexual freedom—for the benefit of the men. In reality not only permitted, but also assiduously practised by the ruling class, it is denounced only nominally. Still in practice this denunciation strikes by no means the men who indulge in it, but only the women. These are ostracised and cast out by society, in order to proclaim once more the fundamental law of unconditional male supremacy over the female sex.

However, a second contradiction is thereby developed within monogamy itself. By the side of the husband, who is making his life pleasant by hetaerism, stands the neglected wife. And you cannot have one side of the contradiction without the other, just as you cannot have the whole apple after eating half of it. Nevertheless this seems to have been the idea of the men, until their wives taught them a lesson. Monogamy introduces two permanent social characters that were formerly unknown: the standing lover of the wife and the cuckold. The men had gained the victory over the women, but the vanquished mag-

THE ORIGIN OF THE FAMILY

nanimously provided the coronation. In addition to monogamy and hetaerism, adultery became an unavoidable social institution—denounced, severely punished, but irrepressible. The certainty of paternal parentage rested as of old on moral conviction at best, and in order to solve the unreconcilable contradiction, the code Napoléon decreed in its article 312: "L'enfant conçu pendant le mariage a pour père le mari;" the child conceived during marriage has for its father—the husband. This is the last result of three thousand years of monogamy.

Thus we have in the monogamous family, at least in those cases that remain true to historical development and clearly express the conflict between man and wife created by the exclusive supremacy of men, a miniature picture of the contrasts and contradictions of society at large. Split by class-differences since the beginning of civilization, society has been unable to reconcile and overcome these antitheses. Of course, I am referring here only to those cases of monogamy, where matrimonial life actually remains in accord with the original character of the whole institution, but where the wife revolts against the rule of the man. Nobody knows better than your German philistine that not all marriages follow such a course. He does not understand how to maintain the control of his own home any better than that of the State, and his wife is, therefore, fully entitled to wearing the trousers, which he does not deserve. But he thinks himself far superior to his French companion in misery, who more frequently fares far worse.

The monogamous family, by the way, did not everywhere and always appear in the classic severe form it had among the Greeks. Among the Romans, who as future conquerors of the world had a sharper although less refined eye than the Greeks, the women

THE FAMILY

were freer and more respected. A Roman believed that the conjugal faith of his wife was sufficiently safeguarded by his power over her life and death. Moreover, the women could voluntarily dissolve the marriage as well as the men. But the highest progress in the development of monogamy was doubtless due to the entrance of the Germans into history, probably because on account of their poverty their monogamy had not yet fully outgrown the pairing family. Three facts mentioned by Tacitus favor this conclusion: In the first place, although marriage was held very sacred—"they are satisfied with one wife, the women are protected by chastity"—still polygamy was in use among the distinguished and the leaders of the tribes, as was the case in the pairing families of the American Indians. Secondly, the transition from maternal to paternal law could have taken place only a short while before, because the mother's brother—the next male relative in the gens by maternal law—was still considered almost a closer relative than the natural father, also in accordance with the standpoint of the American Indians. The latter furnished to Marx, according to his own testimony, the key to the comprehension of German primeval history. And thirdly, the German women were highly respected and also influenced public affairs, a fact directly opposed to monogamic male supremacy. In all these things the Germans almost harmonize with the Spartans, who, as we saw, also had not fully overcome the pairing family. Hence in this respect an entirely new element succeeded to the world's supremacy with the Germans. The new monogamy now developing the ruins of the Roman world from the mixture of nations endowed male rule with a milder form and accorded to women a position that was at least outwardly far more respected and free than classical antiquity ever knew.

THE ORIGIN OF THE FAMILY

Not until now was there a possibility of developing from monogamy—in it, by the side of it or against it, as the case might be—the highest ethical progress we owe to it: the modern individual sexlove, unknown to all previous ages.

This progress doubtless arose from the fact that the Germans still lived in the pairing family and inoculated monogamy as far as possible with the position of women corresponding to the former. It was in no way due to the legendary and wonderfully pure natural qualities of the Germans. These qualities were limited to the simple fact that the pairing family indeed does not create the marked moral contrasts of monogamy. On the contrary, the Germans, especially those who wandered southeast among the nomadic nations of the Black Sea, had greatly degenerated morally. Beside the equestrian tricks of the inhabitants of the steppe they had also acquired some very unnatural vices. This is expressly confirmed of the Thaifali by Ammianus and of the Heruli by Prokop.

Although monogamy was the only one of all known forms of the family in which modern sexlove could develop, this does not imply that it developed exclusively or even principally as mutual love of man and wife. The very nature of strict monogamy under man's rule excluded this. Among all historically active, i. e., ruling, classes matrimony remained what it had been since the days of the pairing family—a conventional matter arranged by the parents. And the first historical form of sexlove as a passion, as an attribute of every human being (at least of the ruling classes), the specific character of the highest form of the sexual impulse, this first form, the love of the knights in the middle ages, was by no means matrimonial love, but quite the contrary. In its classic form, among the Provencals, it heads with full sails

THE FAMILY

for adultery and their poets extol the latter. The flower of Provençal love poetry, the Albas, describe in glowing colors how the knight sleeps with his adored—the wife of another—while the watchman outside calls him at the first faint glow of the morning (alba) and enables him to escape unnoticed. The poems culminate in the parting scene. Likewise the Frenchmen of the north and also the honest Germans adopted this style of poetry and the manner of knightly love corresponding to it. Old Wolfram von Eschenbach has left us three wonderful "day songs" treating this same questionable subject, and I like them better than his three heroic epics.

Civil matrimony in our day is of two kinds. In Catholic countries, the parents provide a fitting spouse for their son as of old, and the natural consequence is the full development of the contradictions inherent to monogamy: voluptuous hetaerism on the man's part, voluptuous adultery of the woman. Probably the Catholic church has abolished divorce for the simple reason that it had come to the conclusion, there was as little help for adultery as for death. In Protestant countries, again, it is the custom to give the bourgeois son more or less liberty in chosing his mate. Hence a certain degree of love may be at the bottom of such a marriage and for the sake of propriety this is always assumed, quite in keeping with Protestant hypocrisy. In this case hetaerism is carried on less strenuously and adultery on the part of the woman is not so frequent. But as human beings remain under any form of marriage what they were before marrying, and as the citizens of Protestant countries are mostly philistines, this Protestant monogamy on the average of the best cases confines itself to the community of a leaden ennui, labeled wedded bliss. The best mirror of these two species of marriage is the novel, the French

THE ORIGIN OF THE FAMILY

novel for the Catholic, the German novel for the Protestant brand. In both of these novels they "get one another:" in the German novel the man gets the girl, in the French novel the husband gets the horns. It does not always go without saying which of the two deserves the most pity. For this reason the tediousness of the German novels is abhorred as much by the French bourgeois as the "immorality" of the French novels by the German philistine. Of late, since Berlin became cosmopolitan, the German novel begins to treat somewhat timidly of the hetaerism and adultery that a long time ago became familiar features of that city.

In both cases the marriage is influenced by the class environment of the participants, and in this respect it always remains conventional. This conventionalism often enough results in the most pronounced prostitution—sometimes of both parties, more commonly of the women. She is distinguished from a courtisane only in that she does not offer her body for money by the hour like a commodity, but sells it into slavery for once and all. Fourier's words hold good with respect to all conventional marriages: "As in grammar two negatives make one affirmative, so in matrimonial ethics, two prostitutions are considered as one virtue." Sexual love in man's relation to woman becomes and can become the rule among the oppressed classes alone, among the proletarians of our day—no matter whether this relation is officially sanctioned or not.

Here all the fundamental conditions of classic monogamy have been abolished. Here all property is missing and it was precisely for the protection and inheritance of this that monogamy and man rule were established. Hence all incentive to make this rule felt is wanting here. More still, the funds are missing. Civil law protecting male rule applies only to

THE FAMILY

the possessing classes and their intercourse with proletarians. Law is expensive and therefore the poverty of the laborer makes it meaningless for his relation to his wife. Entirely different personal and social conditions decide in this case. And finally, since the great industries have removed women from the home to the labor market and to the factory, the last remnant of man rule in the proletarian home has lost its ground—except, perhaps, a part of the brutality against women that has become general since the advent of monogamy. Thus the family of the proletarian is no longer strictly monogamous, even with all the most passionate love and the most unalterable loyalty of both parties, and in spite of any possible clerical or secular sanction. Consequently the eternal companions of monogamy, hetaerism and adultery, play an almost insignificant role here. The woman has practically regained the right of separation, and if a couple cannot agree, they rather separate. In short, the proletarian marriage is monogamous in the etymological sense of the word, but by no means in a historical sense.

True, our jurists hold that the progress of legislation continually lessens all cause of complaint for women. The modern systems of civil law recognize, first that marriage, in order to be legal, must be a contract based on voluntary consent of both parties, and secondly that during marriage the relations of both parties shall be founded on equal rights and duties. These two demands logically enforced will, so they claim, give to women everything they could possibly ask.

This genuinely juridical argumentation is exactly the same as that used by the radical republican bourgeois to cut short and dismiss the proletarian. The labor contract is said to be voluntarily made by both parties. But it is considered as voluntary when the

THE ORIGIN OF THE FAMILY

law places both parties on equal terms on paper. The power conferred on one party by the division of classes, the pressure thereby exerted on the other party, the actual economic relation of the two—all this does not concern the law. Again, during the term of the contract both parties are held to have equal rights, unless one has expressly renounced his right. That the economic situation forces the laborer to give up even the last semblance of equality, that is not the fault of the law.

In regard to marriage, even the most advanced law is completely satisfied after both parties have formally declared their willingness. What passes behind the juridical scenes where the actual process of living is going on, and how this willingness is brought about, that cannot be the business of the law and the jurist. Yet the simplest legal comparison should show to the jurist what this willingness really means. In those countries where a legitimate portion of the parental wealth is assured to children and where these cannot be disinherited—in Germany, in countries with French law, etc.—the children are bound to secure the consent of their parents for marrying. In countries with English law, where the consent of the parents is by no means a legal qualification of marriage, the parents have full liberty to bequeath their wealth to anyone and may disinherit their children at will. Hence it is clear that among classes having any property to bequeath the freedom to marry is not a particle greater in England and America than in France and Germany.

The legal equality of man and woman in marriage is by no means better founded. Their legal inequality inherited from earlier stages of society is not the cause, but the effect of the economic oppression of women. In the ancient communistic household comprising many married couples and their children, the

THE FAMILY

administration of the household entrusted to women was just as much a public function, a socially necessary industry, as the procuring of food by men. In the patriarchal and still more in the monogamous family this was changed. The administration of the household lost its public character. It was no longer a concern of society. It became a private service. The woman became the first servant of the house, excluded from participation in social production. Only by the great industries of our time the access to social production was again opened for women— for proletarian women alone, however. This is done in such a manner that they remain excluded from public production and cannot earn anything, if they fulfill their duties in the private service of the family; or that they are unable to attend to their family duties, if they wish to participate in public industries and earn a living independently. As in the factory, so women are situated in all business departments up to the medical and legal professions. The modern monogamous family is founded on the open or disguised domestic slavery of women, and modern society is a mass composed of molecules in the form of monogamous families. In the great majority of cases the man has to earn a living and to support his family, at least among the possessing classes. He thereby obtains a superior position that has no need of any legal special privilege. In the family, he is the bourgeois, the woman represents the proletariat. In the industrial world, however, the specific character of the economic oppression weighing on the proletariat appears in its sharpest outlines only after all special privileges of the capitalist class are abolished and the full legal equality of both classes is established. A democratic republic does not abolish the distinction between the two classes. On the contrary, it offers the battleground on which this dis-

THE ORIGIN OF THE FAMILY

tinction can be fought out. Likewise the peculiar character of man's rule over woman in the modern family, the necessity and the manner of accomplishing the real social equality of the two, will appear in broad daylight only then, when both of them will enjoy complete legal equality. It will then be seen that the emancipation of women is primarily dependent on the re-introduction of the whole female sex into the public industries. To accomplish this, the monogamous family must cease to be the industrial unit of society.

* * * * * * * * * *

We have, then, three main forms of the family, corresponding in general to the three main stages of human development. For savagery group marriage, for barbarism the pairing family, for civilization monogamy supplemented by adultery and prostitution. Between the pairing family and monogamy, in the higher stage of barbarism, the rule of men over female slaves and polygamy is inserted.

As we proved by our whole argument, the progress visible in this chain of phenomena is connected with the peculiarity of more and more curtailing the sexual freedom of the group marriage for women, but not for men. And group marriage is actually practised by men to this day. What is considered a crime for women and entails grave legal and social consequences for them, is considered honorable for men or in the worst case a slight moral blemish born with pleasure. But the more traditional hetaerism is changed in our day by capitalistic production and conforms to it, the more hetaerism is transformed into undisguised prostitution, the more demoralizing are its effects. And it demoralizes men far more than women. Prostitution does not degrade the whole female sex, but only the luckless women that become its victims, and even those not

THE FAMILY

to the extent generally assumed. But it degrades the character of the entire male world. Especially a long engagement is in nine cases out of ten a perfect training school of adultery.

We are now approaching a social revolution, in which the old economic foundations of monogamy will disappear just as surely as those of its complement, prostitution. Monogamy arose through the concentration of considerable wealth in one hand—a man's hand—and from the endeavor to bequeath this wealth to the children of this man to the exclusion of all others. This necessitated monogamy on the woman's, but not on the man's part. Hence this monogamy of women in no way hindered open or secret polygamy of men. Now, the impending social revolution will reduce this whole care of inheritance to a minimum by changing at least the overwhelming part of permanent and inheritable wealth—the means of production—into social property. Since monogamy was caused by economic conditions, will it disappear when these causes are abolished?

One might reply, not without reason: not only will it not disappear, but it will rather be perfectly realized. For with the transformation of the means of production into collective property, wagelabor will also disappear, and with it the proletariat and the necessity for a certain, statistically ascertainable number of women to surrender for money. Prostitution disappears and monogamy, instead of going out of existence, at last becomes a reality—for men also.

At all events, the situation will be very much changed for men. But also that of women, and of all women, will be considerably altered. With the transformation of the means of production into collective property the monogamous family ceases to be the economic unit of society. The private household changes to a social industry. The care and educa-

THE ORIGIN OF THE FAMILY

tion of children becomes a public matter. Society cares equally well for all children, legal or illegal. This removes the care about the "consequences" which now forms the essential social factor—moral and economic—hindering a girl to surrender unconditionally to the beloved man. Will not this be sufficient cause for a gradual rise of a more unconventional intercourse of the sexes and a more lenient public opinion regarding virgin honor and female shame? And finally, did we not see that in the modern world monogamy and prostitution, though antitheses, are inseparable and poles of the same social condition? Can prostitution disappear without engulfing at the same time monogamy?

Here a new element becomes active, an element which at best existed only in the germ at the time when monogamy developed: individual sexlove.

Before the middle ages we cannot speak of individual sexlove. It goes without saying that personal beauty, intimate intercourse, harmony of inclinations, etc., awakened a longing for sexual intercourse in persons of different sex, and that it was not absolutely immaterial to men and women, with whom they entered into such most intimate intercourse. But from such a relation to our sexlove there is a long way yet. All through antiquity marriages were arranged for the participants by the parents, and the former quietly submitted. What little matrimonial love was known to antiquity was not subjective inclination, but objective duty; not cause, but corollary of marriage. Love affairs in a modern sense occurred in classical times only outside of official society. The shepherds whose happiness and woe in love is sung by Theocritos and Moschus, such as Daphnis and Chloë of Longos, all these were slaves who had no share in the state and in the daily sphere of the free citizen. Outside of slave circles we find

THE FAMILY

love affairs only as products of disintegration of the sinking old world. Their objects are women who also are standing outside of official society, hetaerae that are either foreigners or liberated slaves: in Athens since the beginning of its decline, in Rome at the time of the emperors. If love affairs really occurred between free male and female citizens, it was only in the form of adultery. And to the classical love poet of antiquity, the old Anakreon, sexlove in our sense was so immaterial, that he did not even care a fig for the sex of the beloved being.

Our sexlove is essentially different from the simple sexual craving, the Eros, of the ancients. In the first place it presupposes mutual love. In this respect woman is the equal of man, while in the antique Eros her permission is by no means always asked. In the second place our sexlove has such a degree of intensity and duration that in the eyes of both parties lack of possession and separation appear as a great, if not the greatest, calamity. In order to possess one another they play for high stakes, even to the point of risking their lives, a thing heard of only in adultery during the classical age. And finally a new moral standard is introduced for judging sexual intercourse. We not only ask: "Was it legal or illegal?" but also: "Was it caused by mutual love or not?" Of course, this new standard meets with no better fate in feudal or bourgeois practice than all other moral standards—it is simply ignored. But neither does it fare worse. It is recognized just as much as the others—in theory, on paper. And that is all we can expect at present.

Where antiquity left off with its attempts at sexual love, there the middle ages resumed the thread: with adultery. We have already described the love of the knights that invented the day songs. From this love endeavoring to break through the bonds of marriage

THE ORIGIN OF THE FAMILY

to the love destined to found marriage, there is a long distance which was never fully traversed by the knights. Even in passing on from the frivolous Romanic race to the virtuous Germans, we find in the Nibelungen song Kriemhild, who secretly is no less in love with Siegfried than he with her, meekly replying to Gunther's announcement that he has pledged her in troth to a certain knight whom he does not name: "You need not beg for my consent; as you will demand, so I shall ever be; whomever you, sir, will select for my husband, I shall willingly take in troth." It does not enter her head at all that her love could find any consideration. Gunther asks for Brunhild, Etzel for Kriemhild without ever having seen one another. The same is true of the suit of Gutrun Sigebant of Ireland for the Norwegian Ute and of Hetel of Hegelingen for Hilda of Ireland. When Siegfried of Morland, Hartmut of Oranien and Herwig of Sealand court Gutrun, then it happens for the first time that the lady voluntarily decides, favoring the last named knight. As a rule the bride of the young prince is selected by his parents. Only when the latter are no longer alive, he chooses his own bride with the advice of the great feudal lords who in all cases of this kind have a decisive voice. Nor could it be otherwise. For the knight and the baron as well as for the ruler of the realm himself, marriage is a political act, an opportunity for increasing their power by new federations. The interest of the house must decide, not the arbitrary inclination of the individual. How could love have a chance to decide the question of marriage in the last instance under such conditions?

The same held good for the bourgeois of the medieval towns, the members of the guilds. Precisely the privileges protcting them, the clauses and restrictions of the guild charters, the artificial lines of di-

THE FAMILY

vision separating them legally, here from the other guilds, there from their journeymen and apprentices, drew a sufficiently narrow circle for the selection of a fitting bourgeois spouse. Under such a complicated system, the question of fitness was unconditionally decided, not by individual inclination, but by family interests.

In the overwhelming majority of cases the marriage contract thus remained to the end of the middle ages what it had been from the outset: a matter that was not decided by the parties most interested. In the beginning one was already married from his birth—married to a whole group of the other sex. In the later forms of group marriage, a similar relation was probably maintained, only under a continual narrowing of the group. In the pairing family it is the rule for mothers to exchange mutual pledges for the marriage of their children. Here also the main consideration is given to new ties of relationship that will strengthen the position of the young couple in the gens and the tribe. And when with the preponderance of private property over collective property and with the interest for inheritance paternal law and monogamy assumed the supremacy, then marriage became still more dependent on economic considerations. The form of purchase marriage disappears, but the essence of the transaction is more and more intensified, so that not only the woman, but also the man have a fixed price—not according to his qualities, but to his wealth. That mutual fondness of the marrying parties should be the one factor dominating all others had always been unheard of in the practice of the ruling classes. Such a thing occurred at best in romances or—among the oppressed classes that were not counted.

This was the situation encountered by capitalist production when it began to prepare, since the epoch

THE ORIGIN OF THE FAMILY

of geographical discoveries, for the conquest of the world by international trade and manufacture. One would think that this mode of making the marriage contract would have been extremely acceptable to capitalism, and it was. And yet—the irony of fate is inexplicable—capitalist production had to make the decisive breach through this mode. By changing all things into commodities, it dissolved all inherited and traditional relations and replaced time hallowed custom and historical right by purchase and sale, by the "free contract." And the English jurist, H. S. Maine, thought he had made a stupendous discovery by saying that our whole progress over former epochs consisted in arriving from status to contract, from inherited to voluntarily contracted conditions. So far as this is correct, it had already been mentioned in the Communist Manifesto.

But in order to make contracts, people must have full freedom over their persons, actions and possessions. They must furthermore be on terms of mutual equality. The creation of these "free" and "equal" people was precisely one of the main functions of capitalistic production. What though this was done at first in a half-conscious way and, moreover, in a religious disguise? Since the Lutheran and Calvinist reformation the thesis was accepted that a human being is fully responsible for his actions only then, when these actions were due to full freedom of will. And it was held to be a moral duty to resist any compulsion for an immoral action. How did this agree with the prevailing practice of match-making? Marriage according to bourgeois conception was a contract, a legal business affair, and the most important one at that, because it decided the weal and woe of body and spirit of two beings for life. At that time the agreement was formally voluntary; without the consent of the contracting parties nothing could be

THE FAMILY

done. But it was only too well known how this consent was obtained and who were really the contracting parties. If, however, perfect freedom of decision is demanded for all other contracts, why not for this one? Did not the two young people who were to be coupled together have the right freely to dispose of themselves, of their bodies and the organs of these? Had not sexual love become the custom through the knights and was not, in opposition to knightly adultery, the love of married couples its proper bourgeois form? And if it was the duty of married couples to love one another, was it not just as much the duty of lovers to marry each other and nobody else? Stood not the right of lovers higher than the right of parents, relatives and other customary marriage brokers and matrimonial agents? If the right of free personal investigation made its way unchecked into the church and religion, how could it bear with the insupportable claims of the older generation on the body, soul, property, happiness and misfortune of the younger generation?

These questions had to be raised at a time when all the old ties of society were loosened and all traditional conceptions tottering. The size of the world had increased tenfold at a bound. Instead of one quadrant of one hemisphere, the whole globe now spread before the eyes of West Europeans who hastened to take possession of the other seven quadrants. And the thousand-year-old barriers of conventional medieval thought fell like the old narrow obstacles to marriage. An infinitely wider horizon opened out before the outer and inner eyes of humanity. What mattered the well-meaning propriety, what the honorable privilege of the guild overcome through generations to the young man tempted by the gold and silver mines of Mexico and Potosi?

It was the knight errant time of the bourgeoisie.

THE ORIGIN OF THE FAMILY

It had its own romances and love dreams, but on a bourgeois footing and, in the last instance, with bourgeois aims.

Thus it came about that the rising bourgeoisie more and more recognized the freedom of contracting in marriage and carried it through in the manner described above, especially in Protestant countries, where existing institutions were most strongly shaken. Marriage remained class marriage, but within the class a certain freedom of choice was accorded to the contracting parties. And on paper, in moral theory as in poetical description, nothing was more unalterably established than the idea that every marriage was immoral unless founded on mutual sex-love and perfectly free agreement of husband and wife. In short, the love match was proclaimed as a human right, not only as droit de l'homme—man's right—but also for once as droit de femme—woman's right.

However, this human right differed from all other so-called human rights in one respect. While in practice other rights remained the privileges of the ruling class, the bourgeoisie, and were directly or indirectly curtailed for proletarians, the irony of history once more asserted itself in this case. The ruling class remains subject to well-known economic influences and, therefore, shows marriage by free selection only in exceptional cases. But among the oppressed class, love matches are the rule, as we have seen.

Hence the full freedom of marriage can become general only after all minor economic considerations, that still exert such a powerful influence on the choice of a mate for life, have been removed by the abolition of capitalistic production and of the property relations created by it. Then no other motive will remain but mutual fondness.

THE FAMILY

Since sexlove is exclusive by its very nature—although this exclusiveness is at present realized for women alone—marriage founded on sexlove must be monogamous. We have seen that Bachofen was perfectly right in regarding the progress from group marriage to monogamy mainly as the work of women. Only the advance from the pairing family to monogamy must be charged to the account of men. This advance implied, historically, a deterioration in the position of women and a greater opportunity for men to be faithless. Remove the economic considerations that now force women to submit to the customary disloyalty of men, and you will place women on a equal footing with men. All present experiences prove that this will tend much more strongly to make men truly monogamous, than to make women polyandrous.

However, those peculiarities that were stamped upon the face of monogamy by its rise through property relations, will decidedly vanish, namely the supremacy of men and the indissolubility of marriage. The supremacy of man in marriage is simply the consequence of his economic superiority and will fall with the abolition of the latter.

The indissolubility of marriage is partly the consequence of economic conditions, under which monogamy arose, partly tradition from the time where the connection between this economic situation and monogamy, not yet clearly understood, was carried to extremes by religion. To-day, it has been perforated a thousand times. If marriage founded on love is alone moral, then it follows that marriage is moral only as long as love lasts. The duration of an attack of individual sexlove varies considerably according to individual disposition, especially in men. A positive cessation of fondness or its replacement by a new passionate love makes a separation a bless-

THE ORIGIN OF THE FAMILY

ing for both parties and for society. But humanity will be spared the useless wading through the mire of a divorce case.

What we may anticipate about the adjustment of sexual relations after the impending downfall of capitalist production is mainly of a negative nature and mostly confined to elements that will disappear. But what will be added? That will be decided after a new generation has come to maturity: a race of men who never in their lives have had any occasion for buying with money or other economic means of power the surrender of a woman; a race of women who have never had any occasion for surrendering to any man for any other reason but love, or for refusing to surrender to their lover from fear of economic consequences. Once such people are in the world, they will not give a moment's thought to what we today believe should be their course. They will follow their own practice and fashion their own public opinion about the individual practice of every person—only this and nothing more.

But let us return to Morgan from whom we moved away a considerable distance. The historical investigation of social institutions developed during the period of civilization exceeds the limits of his book. Hence the vicissitudes of monogamy during this epoch occupy him very briefly. He also sees in the further development of the monogamous family a progress, an approach to perfect equality of the sexes, without considering this aim fully realized. But he says: "When the fact is accepted that the family has passed through four successive forms, and is now in a fifth, the question at once arises whether this form can be permanent in the future. The only answer that can be given is that it must advance as society advances, and and change as society changes, even as it has done in the past. It is the creature of the

THE FAMILY

social system, and will reflect its culture. As the monogamian family has improved greatly since the commencement of civilization, and very sensibly in modern times, it is at least supposable that it is capable of still farther improvement until the equality of the sexes is attained. Should the monogamian family in the distant future fail to answer the requirements of society, assuming the continuous progress of civilization, it is impossible to predict the nature of its successor."

CHAPTER III.

THE IROQUOIS GENS.

We now come to another discovery of Morgan that is at least as important as the reconstruction of the primeval form of the family from the systems of kinship. It is the proof that the sex organizations within the tribe of North American Indians, designated by animal names, are essentially identical with the genea of the Greeks and the gentes of the Romans; that the American form is the original from which the Greek and Roman forms were later derived; that the whole organization of Greek and Roman society during primeval times in gens, phratry and tribe finds its faithful parallel in that of the American Indians; that the gens is an institution common to all barbarians up to the time of civilization—at least so far as our present sources of information reach. This demonstration has cleared at a single stroke the most difficult passages of remotest ancient Greek and Roman history. At the same time it has given us unexpected information concerning the fundamental outlines of the constitution of society in primeval times—before the introduction of the state. Simple as the matter is after we have once found it out, still it was only lately discovered by Morgan. In his work of 1871 he had not yet unearthed this mystery. Its revelation has completely silenced for the time being those generally so overconfident English authorities on primeval history.

The Latin word gens, used by Morgan generally for the designation of this sex organization, is derived,

THE IROQUOIS GENS

like the equivalent Greek word genos, from the common Aryan root gan, signifying to beget. Gens, genos, Sanskrit dschanas, Gothic kuni, ancient Norse and Anglesaxon kyn, English kin, Middle High German künne, all signify lineage, descent. Gens in Latin, genos in Greek, specially designate that sex organization which boasted of common descent (from a common sire) and was united into a separate community by certain social and religious institutions, but the origin and nature of which nevertheless remained obscure to all our historians.

Elsewhere, in speaking of the Punaluan family, we saw how the gens was constituted in its original form. It consisted of all individuals who by means of the Punaluan marriage and in conformity with the conceptions necessarily arising in it made up the recognized offspring of a certain ancestral mother, the founder of that gens. Since fatherhood is uncertain in this form of the family, female lineage is alone valid. And as brothers must not marry their sisters, but only women of foreign descent, the childred bred from these foreign women do not belong to the gens, according to maternal law. Hence only the offspring of the daughters of every generation remain in the same sex organization. The descendants of the sons are transferred to the gentes of the new mothers. What becomes of this group of kinship when it constitutes itself a separate group, distinct from similar groups in the same tribe?

As the classical form of this original gens Morgan selects that of the Iroquois, more especially that of the Seneca tribe. This tribe has eight gentes named after animals: 1. Wolf. 2. Bear. 3. Turtle. 4. Beaver. 5. Deer. 6. Snipe. 7. Heron. 8. Hawk. Every gens observes the following customs:

1. The gens elects its sachem (official head during peace) and its chief (leader in war). The sachem

THE ORIGIN OF THE FAMILY

must be selected within the gens and his office was in a sense hereditary. It had to be filled immediately after a vacancy occurred. The chief could be selected outside of the gens, and his office could even be temporarily vacant. The son never followed his father in the office of sachem, because the Iroquois observed maternal law, in consequence of which the son belonged to another gens. But the brother or the son of a sister was often elected as a successor. Men and women both voted in elections. The election, however, had to be confirmed by the other seven gentes, and then only the sachem-elect was solemnly invested, by the common council of the whole Iroquois federation. The significance of this will be seen later. The power of the sachem within the tribe was of a paternal, purely moral nature. He had no means of coercion at his command. He was besides by virtue of his office a member of the tribal council of the Senecas and of the federal council of the whole Iroquois nation. The Chief had the right to command only in times of war.

2. The gens can retire the sachem and the chief at will. This again is done by men and women jointly. The retired men are considered simple warriors and private persons like all others. The tribal council, by the way, can also retire the sachems, even against the will of the tribe.

3. No member is permitted to marry within the gens. This is the fundamental rule of the gens, the tie that holds it together. It is the negative expression of the very positive blood relationship, by virtue of which the individuals belonging to it become a gens. By the discovery of this simple fact Morgan for the first time revealed the nature of the gens. How little the gens had been understood before him is proven by former reports on savages and barbarians, in which the different organizations of which

THE IROQUOIS GENS

the gentile order is composed are jumbled together without understanding and distinction as tribe, clan, thum, etc. Sometimes it is stated that intermarrying within these organizations is forbidden. This gave rise to the hopeless confusion, in which McLennan could pose as Napoleon and establish order by the decree: All tribes are divided into those that forbid intermarrying (exogamous) and those that permit it (endogamous). And after he had thus made confusion worse confounded, he could indulge in deep meditations which of his two preposterous classes was the older: exogamy or endogamy. By the discovery of the gens founded on affinity of blood and the resulting impossibility of its members to intermarry, this nonsense found a natural end. It is self understood that the marriage interdict within the gens was strictly observed at the stage in which we find the Iroquois.

4. The property of deceased members fell to the share of the other gentiles; it had to remain in the gens. In view of the insignificance of the objects an Iroquois could leave behind, the nearest gentile relations divided the heritage. Was the deceased a man, then his natural brothers, sisters and the brothers of the mother shared in his property. Was it a woman, then her children and natural sisters shared, but not her brothers. For this reason husband and wife could not inherit from one another, nor the children from the father.

5. The gentile members owed to each other help, protection and especially assistance in revenging injury inflicted by strangers. The individual relied for his protection on the gens and could be assured of it. Whoever injured the individual, injured the whole gens. From this blood kinship arose the obligation to blood revenge that was unconditionally recognized by the Iroquois. If a stranger killed a gentile

THE ORIGIN OF THE FAMILY

member, the whole gens of the slain man was pledged to revenge his death. First mediation was tried. The gens of the slayer deliberated and offered to the gentile council of the slain propositions for atonement, consisting generally in expressions of regret and presents of considerable value. If these were accepted, the matter was settled. In the opposite case the injured gens appointed one or more avengers who were obliged to pursue the slayer and to kill him. If they succeeded, the gens of the slayer had no right to complain. The account was squared.

6. The gens had certain distinct names or series of names, which no other gens in the whole tribe could use, so that the name of the individual indicated to what gens he belonged. A gentile name at the same time bestowed gentile rights.

7. The gens may adopt strangers who thereby are adopted into the whole tribe. The prisoners of war who were not killed became by adoption into a gens tribal members of the Senecas and thus received full gentile and tribal rights. The adoption took place on the motion of some gentile members, of men who accepted the stranger as a brother or sister, of women who accepted him as a child. The solemn introduction into the gens was necessary to confirm the adoption. Frequently certain gentes that had shrunk exceptionally were thus strengthened by mass adoptions from another gens with the consent of the latter. Among the Iroquois the solemn introduction into the gens took place in a public meeting of the tribal council, whereby it actually became a religious ceremony.

The existence of special religious celebrations among Indian gentes can hardly be demonstrated. But the religious rites of the Indians are more or less connected with the gens. At the six annual religious festivals of the Iroquois the sachems and chiefs of

THE IROQUOIS GENS

the different gentes were added to the "Keepers of the Faith" and had the functions of priests.

9. The gens had a common burial place. Among the Iroquois of the State of New York, who are crowded by white men all around them, the burial place has disappeared, but it existed formerly. Among other Indians it is still in existence, e. g., among the Tuscaroras, near relatives of the Iroquois, where every gens has a row by itself in the burial place, although they are Christians. The mother is buried in the same row as her children, but not the father. And among the Iroquois the whole gens of the deceased attends the funeral, prepares the grave and provides the addresses, etc.

10. The gens had a council, the democratic assembly of all male and female gentiles of adult age, all with equal suffrage. This council elected and deposed its sachems and chiefs; likewise the other "Keepers of the Faith." It deliberated on gifts of atonement or blood revenge for murdered gentiles and it adopted strangers into the gens. In short, it was the sovereign power in the gens.

The following are the rights and privileges of the typical Indian gens, according to Morgan: "All the members of an Iroquois gens were personally free, and they were bound to defend each other's freedom; they were equal in privileges and in personal rights, the sachems and chiefs claiming no superiority; and they were a brotherhood bound together by ties of kin. Liberty, equality and fraternity, though never formulated, were cardinal principles of the gens. These facts are material, because the gens was the unit of a social and governmental system, the foundation upon which Indian society was organized. A structure composed of such units would of necessity bear the impress of their character, for as the unit, so the compound. It serves to explain that sense

THE ORIGIN OF THE FAMILY

of independence and personal dignity universally at attribute of Indian character."

At the time of the discovery the Indians of entire North America were organized in gentes by maternal law. Only "in some tribes, as among the Dakotas, the gentes had fallen out; in others as among the Ojibwas, the Omahas and the Mayas of Yucatan, descent had been changed from the female to the male line."

Among many Indian tribes with more than five or six gentes we find three, four or more gentes united into a separate group, called phratry by Morgan in accurate translation of the Indian name by its Greek equivalent. Thus the Senecas have two phratries, the first comprising gentes one to four, the second gentes five to eight. Closer investigation shows that these phratries generally represent the original gentes that formed the tribe in the beginning. For the marriage interdict necessitated the existence of at least two gentes in a tribe in order to realize its separate existence. As the tribe increased, every gens segmented into two or more new gentes, while the original gens comprising all the daughter gentes, lived on in the phratry. Among the Senecas and most of the other Indians "the gentes in the same phratry are brother gentes to each other, and cousin gentes to those of the other phratry"—terms that have a very real and expressive meaning in the American system of kinship, as we have seen. Originally no Seneca was allowed to marry within his phratry, but this custom has long become obsolete and is now confined to the gens. According to the tradition among the Senecas, the bear and the deer were the two original gentes, from which the others were formed by segmentation. After this new institution had become well established it was modified according to circumstances. If certain gentes became extinct, it

THE IROQUOIS GENS

sometimes happened that by mutual consent the members of one gens were transferred in a body from other phratries. Hence we find the gentes of the same name differently grouped in the phratries of the different tribes.

"The phratry, among the Iroquois, was partly for social and partly for religious objects." 1. In the ball game one phratry plays against another. Each one sends its best players, the other members, upon different sides of the field, watch the game and bet against one another on the result. 2. In the tribal council the sachems and chiefs of each phratry are seated opposite one another, every speaker addressing the representatives of each phratry as separate bodies. 3. When a murder had been committed in the tribe, the slayer and the slain belonging to different phratries, the injured gens often appealed to its brother gentes. These held a phratry council which in a body addressed itself to the other phratry, in order to prevail on the latter to assemble in council and effect a condonation of the matter. In this case the phratry re-appears in its original gentile capacity, and with a better prospect of success than the weaker gens, its daughter. 4. At the funeral of prominent persons the opposite phratry prepared the interment and the burial rites, while the phratry of the deceased attended the funeral as mourners. If a sachem died, the opposite phratry notified the central council of the Iroquois that the office of the deceased had become vacant. 5. In electing a sachem the phratry council also came into action. Endorsement by the brother gentes was generally considered a matter of fact, but the gentes of the other phratry might oppose. In such a case the council of this phratry met, and if it maintained its opposition, the election was null and void. 6. Formerly the Iroquois had special relig-

THE ORIGIN OF THE FAMILY

ious mysteries, called medicine lodges by the white men. These mysteries were celebrated among the Senecas by two religious societies that had a special form of initiation for new members; each phratry was represented by one of these societies. 7. If, as is almost certain, the four lineages occupying the four quarters of Tlascalá at the time of the conquest were four phratries, then it is proved that the phratries were at the same time military units, as were the Greek phratries and similar sex organizations of the Germans. Each of these four lineages went into battle as a separate group with its special uniform and flag and its own leader.

Just as several gentes form a phratry so in the classical form several phratries form a tribe. In some cases the middle group, the phratry, is missing in strongly decimated tribes.

What constitutes an Indian tribe in America? 1. A distinct territory and a distinct name. Every tribe had a considerable hunting and fishing ground beside the place of its actual settlement. Beyond this territory there was a wide neutral strip of land reaching over to the boundaries of the next tribe; a smaller strip between tribes of related languages, a larger between tribes of foreign languages. This corresponds to the boundary forest of the Germans, the desert created by Caesar's Suevi around their territory, the isârnholt (Danish jarnved, Latin limel Danicus) between Danes and Germans, the sachsen wald (Saxon forest) and the Slavish branibor between Slavs and Germans giving the province of Brandenburg its name. The territory thus surrounded by neutral ground was the collective property of a certain tribe, recognized as such by other tribes and defended against the invasion of others. The disadvantage of undefined boundaries became of prac-

THE IROQUOIS GENS

tical importance only after the population had increased considerably.

The tribal names generally seem to be more the result of chance than of intentional selection. In course of time it frequently happened that a tribe designated a neighboring tribe by another name than that chosen by itself. In this manner the Germans received their first historical name from the Celts.

2. A distinct dialect peculiar to this tribe. As a matter of fact the tribe and the dialect are co-extensive. In America, the formation of new tribes and dialects by segmentation was in progress until quite recently, and doubtless it is still going on. Where two weak tribes amalgamated into one, there it exceptionally happened that two closely related dialects were simultaneously spoken in the same tribe. The average strength of American tribes is less than 2,000 members. The Cherokees, however, number about 26,000, the greatest number of Indians in the United States speaking the same dialect.

3. The right to solemnly invest the sachems and chiefs elected by the gentes, and

4. The right to depose them, even against the will of the gens. As these sachems and chiefs are members of the tribal council, these rights of the tribe explain themselves. Where a league of tribes had been formed and all the tribes were represented in a feudal council, the latter exercised these rights.

5. The possession of common religious conceptions (mythology) and rites. "After the fashion of barbarians the American Indians were a religious people." Their mythology has not yet been critically investigated. They materialized their religious conceptions—spirits of all sorts—in human shapes, but the lower stage of barbarism in which they lived, knows nothing as yet of so-called idols. It is a cult of nature and of the elements, in process of evolution

to pantheism. The different tribes had regular festivals with prescribed forms of worship, mainly dances and games. Especially dancing was an essential part of all religious celebrations. Every tribe celebrated by itself.

6. A tribal council for public affairs. It was composed of all the sachems and chiefs of the different gentes, real representatives because they could be deposed at any moment. It deliberated in public, surrounded by the rest of the tribal members, who had a right to take part in the discussions and claim attention. The council decided. As a rule any one present gained a hearing on his demand. The women could also present their views by a speaker of their choice. Among the Iroquois the final resolution had to be passed unanimously, as was also the case in some resolutions of German mark (border) communities. It was the special duty of the tribal council to regulate the relations with foreign tribes. The council received and despatched legations, declared war and made peace. War was carried on principally by volunteers. "Theoretically, each tribe was at war with every other tribe with which it had not formed a treaty of peace."

Expeditions against such enemies were generally organized by certain prominent warriors. They started a war dance, and whoever took part in it thereby declared his intention to join the expedition. Ranks were formed and the march began immediately. The defense of the attacked tribal territory was also generally carried on by volunteers. The exodus and the return of such columns was always the occasion of public festivities. The consent of the tribal council for such expeditions was not required, and was neither asked nor given. This corresponds to the private war expeditions of German followers described by Tacitus. Only these German

THE IROQUOIS GENS

groups of followers had already assumed a more permanent character, forming a standing center organized during peace, around which the other volunteers gathered in case of war. Such war columns were rarely strong in numbers. The most important expeditions of the Indians, even for long distances, were undertaken by insignificant forces. If more than one group joined for a great expedition, every group obeyed its own leader. The uniformity of the campaign plan was secured as well as possible by a council of these leaders. This is the mode of warfare among the Allemani in the fourth century on the Upper Rhine, as described by Ammianus Marcellinus.

7. In some tribes we find a head chief, whose power, however, is limited. He is one of the sachems who has to take provisional measures in cases requiring immediate action, until the council can assemble and decide. He represents a feeble, but generally undeveloped prototype of an official with executive power. The latter, as we shall see, developed in most cases out of the highest war chief.

The great majority of American Indians did not go beyond the league of tribes. With a few tribes of small membership, separated by wide boundary tracts, weakened by unceasing warfare, they occupied an immense territory. Leagues were now and then formed by kindred tribes as the result of momentary necessity and dissolved again under more favorable conditions. But in certain districts, tribes of the same kin had again found their way out of disbandment into permanent federations, making the first step towards the formation of nations. In the United States we find the highest form of such a league among the Iroquois. Emigrating from their settlements west of the Mississippi, where they probably formed a branch of the great Dakota family, they settled at last after long wanderings in the

THE ORIGIN OF THE FAMILY

present state of New York. They had five tribes: Senecas, Cayugas, Onondagas, Oneidas and Mohawks. They lived on fish, venison, and the products of rough gardening, inhabiting villages protected by stockades. Their number never exceeded 20,000, and certain gentes were common to all five tribes. They spoke closely related dialects of the same language and occupied territories contiguous to one another. As this land was won by conquest, it was natural for these tribes to stand together against the expelled former inhabitants. This led, not later than the beginning of the fifteenth century, to a regular "eternal league," a sworn alliance that immediately assumed an aggressive character, relying on its newly won strength. About 1675, at the summit of its power, it had conquered large districts round about and partly expelled the inhabitants, partly made them tributary. The Iroquois League represented the most advanced social organization attained by Indians that had not passed the lower stage of barbarism. This excludes only the Mexicans, New Mexicans and Peruvians.

The fundamental provisions of the league were:

1. Eternal federation of the five consanguineous tribes on the basis of perfect equality and independence in all internal tribal matters. This consanguinity formed the true fundament of the league. Three of these tribes, called father tribes, were brothers to one another; the other two, also mutual brothers, were called son tribes. The three oldest gentes were represented by living members in all five tribes, and these members were all regarded as brothers. Three other gentes were still alive in three tribes, and all of their members called one another brothers. The common language, only modified by variations of dialect, was the expression and proof of their common descent.

THE IROQUOIS GENS

2. The official organ of the league was a federal council of fifty sachems, all equal in rank and prominence. This council had the supreme decision in all federal matters.

3. On founding this league the fifty sachems had been assigned to the different tribes and gentes as holders of new offices created especially for federal purposes. Vacancies were filled by new elections in the gens, and the holders of these offices could be deposed at will. But the right of installation belonged to the federal council.

4. These federal sachems were at the same time sachems of their tribe and had a seat and a vote in the tribal council.

5. All decisions of the federal council had to be unanimous.

6. The votes were cast by tribes, so that every tribe and the council members of each tribe had to vote together in order to adopt a final resolution.

7. Any one of the five tribes could convoke the federal council, but the council could not convene itself.

8. Federal meetings were held publicly in the presence of the assembled people. Every Iroquois could have the word, but the final decision rested with the council.

9. The league had no official head, no executive chief.

10. It had, however, two high chiefs of war, both with equal functions and power (the two "kings" of Sparta, the two consuls of Rome).

This was the whole constitution, under which the Iroquois lived over four hundred years and still live. I have described it more fully after Morgan, because we have here an opportunity for studying the organization of a society that does not yet know a state. The state presupposes a public power of coërcion

THE ORIGIN OF THE FAMILY

separated from the aggregate body of its members. Maurer, with correct intuition, recognized the constitution of the German Mark as a purely social institution, essentially different from that of a state, though furnishing the fundament on which a state constitution could be erected later on. Hence in all of his writings, he traced the gradual rise of the public power of coërcion from and by the side of primordial constitutions of marks, villages, farms and towns. The North American Indians show how an originally united tribe gradually spreads over an immense continent; how tribes by segmentation become nations, whole groups of tribes; how languages change so that they not only become unintelligible to one another, but also lose every trace of former unity; how at the same time one gens splits up into several gentes, how the old mother gentes are preserved in the phratries and how the names of these oldest gentes still remain the same in widely distant and long separated tribes. Wolf and bear still are gentile names in a majority of all Indian tribes. And the above named constitution is essentially applicable to all of them, except that many did not reach the point of forming leagues of related tribes.

But once the gens was given as a social unit, we also see how the whole constitution of gentes, phratries and tribes developed with almost unavoidable necessity—because naturally—from the gens. All three of them are groups of differentiated consanguine relations. Each is complete in itself, arranges its own local affairs and supplements the other groups. And the cycle of functions performed by them includes the aggregate of the public affairs of men in the lower stage of barbarism.

Wherever we find the gens as the social unit of a nation, we are justified in searching for a tribal organization similar to the one described above. And

THE IROQUOIS GENS

whenever sufficient material is at hand, as in Greek and Roman history, there we shall not only find such an organization, but we may also be assured that the comparison with the American sex organizations will assist us in solving the most perplexing doubts and riddles in places where the material forsakes us.

How wonderful this gentile constitution is in all its natural simplicity! No soldiers, gensdarmes and policemen, no nobility, kings, regents, prefects or judges, no prisons, no lawsuits, and still affairs run smoothly. All quarrels and disputes are settled by the entire community involved in them, either the gens or the tribe or the various gentes among themselves. Only in very rare cases the blood revenge is threatened as an extreme measure. Our capital punishment is simply a civilized form of it, afflicted with all the advantages and drawbacks of civilization. Not a vestige of our cumbersome and intricate system of administration is needed, although there are more public affairs to be settled than nowadays: the communistic household is shared by a number of families, the land belongs to the tribe, only the gardens are temporarily assigned to the households. The parties involved in a question settle it and in most cases the hundred-year-old traditions have settled everything beforehand. There cannot be any poor and destitute—the communistic households and the gentes know their duties toward the aged, sick and disabled. All are free and equal—the women included. There is no room yet for slaves, nor for the subjugation of foreign tribes. When about 1651 the Iroquois had vanquished the Eries and the "Neutral Nation," they offered to adopt them into the league on equal terms. Only when the vanquished declined this offer they were driven out of their territory.

What splendid men and women were produced by such a society! All the white men who came into

THE ORIGIN OF THE FAMILY

contact with unspoiled Indians admired the personal dignity, straightforwardness, strength of character and bravery of these barbarians.

We lately received proofs of such bravery in Africa. A few years ago the Zulus, and some months ago the Nubians, both of which tribes still retain the gentile organization, did what no European army can do. Armed only with lances and spears, without any firearms, they advanced under a hail of bullets from breechloaders up to the bayonets of the English infantry—the best of the world for fighting in closed ranks—and threw them into confusion more than once, yea, even forced them to retreat in spite of the immense disparity of weapons, and in spite of the fact that they have no military service and don't know anything about drill. How enduring and able they are, is proved by the complaints of the English who admit that a Kaffir can cover a longer distance in twenty-four hours than a horse. The smallest muscle springs forth, hard and tough like a whiplash, says an English painter.

Such was human society and its members, before the division into classes had taken place. And a comparison of that social condition with the condition of the overwhelming majority of present day society shows the enormous chasm that separates our proletarian and small farmer from the free gentile of old.

That is one side of the question. We must not overlook, however, that this organization was doomed. It did not pass beyond the tribe. The league of tribes marked the beginning of its downfall, as we shall see, and as the attempts of the Iroquois at subjugating others showed. Whatever went beyond the tribe, went outside of gentilism. Where no direct peace treaty existed, there war reigned from tribe to tribe. And this war was carried on with the particular cruelty

THE IROQUOIS GENS

that distinguishes man from other animals, and that was modified later on simply by self-interest.

The gentile constitution in its most flourishing time, such as we saw it in America, presupposed a very undeveloped state of production, hence a population thinly scattered over a wide area. Man was almost completely dominated by nature, a strange and incomprehensible riddle to him. His simple religious conceptions clearly reflect this. The tribe remained the boundary line for man, as well in regard to himself as to strangers outside. The gens, the tribe and their institutions were holy and inviolate. They were a superior power instituted by nature, and the feelings, thoughts and actions of the individual remained unconditionally subject to them. Commanding as the people of this epoch appear to us, nothing distinguishes one from another. They are still attached, as Marx has it, to the navel string of the primordial community.

The power of these natural and spontaneous communities had to be broken, and it was. But it was done by influences that from the very beginning bear the mark of degradation, of a downfall from the simple moral grandeur of the old gentile society. The new system of classes is inaugurated by the meanest impulses: vulgar covetousness, brutal lust, sordid avarice, selfish robbery of common wealth. The old gentile society without classes is undermined and brought to fall by the most contemptible means: theft, violence, cunning, treason. And during all the thousands of years of its existence, the new society has never been anything else but the development of the small minority at the expense of the exploited and oppressed majority. More than ever this is true at present.

CHAPTER IV.

THE GRECIAN GENS.

Greeks, Pelasgians and other nations of the same tribal origin were constituted since prehistoric times on the same systematic plan as the Americans: gens, phratry, tribe, league of tribes. The phratry might be missing, as e. g. among the Dorians; the league of tribes might not be fully developed in every case; but the gens was everywhere the unit. At the time of their entrance into history, the Greeks were on the threshold of civilization. Two full periods of evolution are stretching between the Greeks and the above named American tribes. The Greeks of the heroic age are by so much ahead of the Iroquois. For this reason the Grecian gens no longer retains the archaic character of the Iroquois gens. The stamp of group marriage is becoming rather blurred. Maternal law had given way to paternal lineage. Rising private property had thus made its first opening in the gentile constitution. A second opening naturally followed the first: Paternal law being now in force, the fortune of a wealthy heiress would have fallen to her husband in the case of her marriage. That would have meant the transfer of her wealth from her own gens to that of her husband. In order to avoid this, the fundament of gentile law was shattered. In such a case, the girl was not only permitted, but obliged to intermarry within the gens, in order to retain the wealth in the latter.

According to Grote's History of Greece, the gens of Attica was held together by the following bonds:

1. Common religious rites and priests installed ex-

THE GRECIAN GENS

clusively in honor of a certain divinity, the alleged gentile ancestor, who was designated by a special by-name in this capacity.

2. A common burial ground. (See Demosthenes' Eubulides.)

3. Right of mutual inheritance.

4. Obligation to mutually help, protect and assist one another in case of violence.

5. Mutual right and duty to intermarry in the gens in certain cases, especially for orphaned girls or heiresses.

6. Possession of common property, at least in some cases, and an archon (supervisor) and treasurer elected for this special case.

The phratry united several gentes, but rather loosely. Still we find in it similar rights and duties, especially common religious rites and the right of avenging the death of a phrator. Again, all the phratries of a tribe had certain religious festivals in common that recurred at regular intervals and were celebrated under the guidance of a phylobasileus (tribal head) selected from the ranks of the nobles (eupatrides).

So far Grote. And Marx adds: "The savage (e. g. the Iroquois) is still plainly visible in the Grecian gens." On further investigation we find additional proofs of this. For the Grecian gens has also the following attributes:

7. Paternal Lineage.

8. Prohibition of intermarrying in the gens except in the case of heiresses. This exception formulated as a law clearly proves the validity of the old rule. This is further substantiated by the **universally** accepted custom that a woman in marrying renounced the religious rites of her gens and accepted those of her husband's gens. She was also registered in his phratry. According to this custom and to a famous quotation in Dikaearchos, marriage outside of the gens

THE ORIGIN OF THE FAMILY

was the rule. Becker in "Charikles" directly assumes that nobody was permitted to intermarry in the gens.

9. The right to adopt strangers in the gens. It was exercised by adoption into the family under public formalities; but it was used sparingly.

10. The right to elect and depose the archons. We know that every gens had its archon. As to the heredity of the office, there is no reliable information. Until the end of barbarism, the probability is always against strict heredity. For it is absolutely incompatible with conditions where rich and poor had perfectly equal rights in the gens.

Not alone Grote, but also Niebuhr, Mommsen and all other historians of classical antiquity were foiled by the gens. Though they chronicled many of its distinguishing marks correctly, still they always regarded it as a group of families and thus prevented their understanding the nature and origin of gentes. Under the gentile constitution, the family never was a unit of organization, nor could it be so, because man and wife necessarily belonged to two different gentes. The gens was wholly comprised in the phratry, the phratry in the tribe. But the family belonged half to the gens of the man, and half to that of the woman. Nor does the state recognize the family in public law. To this day, the family has only a place in private law. Yet all historical records take their departure from the absurd supposition, which was considered almost inviolate during the eighteenth century, that the monogamous family, an institution scarcely older than civilization, is the nucleus around which society and state gradually crystallized.

"Mr. Grote will also please note," throws in Marx, "that the gentes, which the Greeks traced to their mythologies, are older than the mythologies. The latter together with their gods and demi-gods were created by the gentes."

THE GRECIAN GENS

Grote is quoted with preference by Morgan as a prominent and quite trustworthy witness. He relates that every Attic gens had a name derived from its alleged ancestor; that before Solon's time, and even after, it was customary for the gentiles (gennêtes) to inherit the fortunes of their intestate deceased; and that in case of murder first the relatives of the victim had the duty and the right to prosecute the criminal, after them the gentiles and finally the phrators. "Whatever we may learn about the oldest Attic laws is founded on the organization in gentes and phratries."

The descent of the gentes from common ancestors has caused the "schoolbred philistines," as Marx has it, much worry. Representing this descent as purely mythical, they are at a loss to explain how the gentes developed out of independent and wholly unrelated families. But this explanation must be given, if they wish to explain the existence of the gentes. They then turn around in a circle of meaningless gibberish and do not get beyond the phrase: the pedigree is indeed a fable, but the gens is a reality. Grote finally winds up—the parenthetical remarks are by Marx: "We rarely hear about this pedigree, because it is used in public only on certain very festive occasions. But the less prominent gentes had their common religious rites (very peculiar, Mr. Grote!) and their common superhuman ancestor and pedigree just like the more prominent gentes (how very peculiar this, Mr. Grote, in less prominent gentes!); and the ground plan and the ideal fundament (my dear sir! Not ideal, but carnal, anglice "fleshly") was the same in all of them."

Marx sums up Morgan's reply to this as follows: "The system of consanguinity corresponding to the archaic form of the gens—which the Greeks once possessed like other mortals—preserved the knowledge of the mutual relation of all members of the gens.

THE ORIGIN OF THE FAMILY

They learned this important fact by practice from early childhood. With the advent of the monogamous family this was gradually forgotten. The gentile name created a pedigree by the side of which that of the monogamous family seemed insignificant. This name had now the function of preserving the memory of the common descent of its bearers. But the pedigree of the gens went so far back that the gentiles could no longer actually ascertain their mutual kinship, except in a limited number of more recent common ancestors. The name itself was the proof of a common descent and sufficed always except in cases of adoption. To actually dispute all kinship between gentiles after the manner of Grote and Niebuhr, who thus transform the gens into a purely hypothetical and fictitious creation of the brain, is indeed worthy of "ideal" scientists, that is book worms. Because the relation of the generations, especially on the advent of monogamy, is removed to the far distance, and the reality of the past seems reflected in phantastic imaginations, therefore the brave old philistines concluded and conclude that the imaginary pedigree created real gentes!"

The phratry was, as among the Americans, a mothergens comprising several daughter gentes, and often traced them all to the same ancestor. According to Grote "all contemporaneous members of the phratry of Hekataeos were descendants in the sixteenth degree of one and the same divine ancestor. All the gentes of this phratry were therefore literally brother gentes. The phratry is mentioned by Homer as a military unit in that famous passage where Nestor advises Agamemnon: "Arrange the men by phratries and tribes so that phratry may assist phratry, and tribe the tribe." The phratry has the right and the duty to prosecute the death of a phrator, hence in former times the duty of blood revenge. It has,

THE GRECIAN GENS

furthermore, common religious rites and festivals. As a matter of fact, the development of the entire Grecian mythology from the traditional old Aryan cult of nature was essentially due to the gentes and phratries and took place within them. The phratry had an official head (phratriarchos) and also, according to De Coulanges, meetings and binding resolutions, a jurisdiction and administration. Even the state of a later period, while ignoring the gens, left certain public functions to the phratry.

The tribe consisted of several kindred phratries. In Attica there were four tribes of three phratries each; the number of gentes in each phratry was thirty. Such an accurate division of groups reveals the fact of a conscious and well-planned interference with the natural order. How, when and why this was done is not disclosed by Grecian history. The historical memory of the Greeks themselves does not reach beyond the heroic age.

Closely packed in a comparatively small territory as the Greeks were, their dialectic differences were less conspicuous than those developed in the wide American forests. Yet even here we find only tribes of the same main dialect united in a larger organization. Little Attica had its own dialect which later on became the prevailing language in Grecian prose.

In the epics of Homer we generally find the Greek tribes combined into small nations, but so that their gentes, phratries and tribes retained their full independence. They already lived in towns fortified by walls. The population increased with the growth of the herds, with agriculture and the beginnings of the handicrafts. At the same time the differences in wealth became more marked and gave rise to an aristocratic element within the old primordial democracy. The individual little nations carried on an unceasing warfare for the possession of the best land and also

THE ORIGIN OF THE FAMILY

for the sake of looting. Slavery of the prisoners of war was already well established.

The constitution of these tribes and nations was as follows:

1. A permanent authority was the council (bule), originally composed of the gentile archons, but later on, when their number became too great, recruited by selection in such a way that the aristocratic element was developed and strengthened. Dionysios openly speaks of the council at the time of the heroes as being composed of nobles (kratistoi). The council had the final decision in all important matters. In Aeschylos, e. g. the council of Thebes decides that the body of Eteokles be buried with full honors, the body of Polynikes, however, thrown out to be devoured by the dogs. With the rise of the state this council was transformed into the senate.

2. The public meeting (agora). We saw how the Iroquois, men and women, attended the council meetings, taking an orderly part in the discussions and influencing them. Among the Homeric Greeks, this attendance had developed to a complete public meeting. This was also the case with the Germans of the archaic period. The meeting was called by the council. Every man could demand the word. The final vote was taken by hand raising (Aeschylos in "The Suppliants," 607), or by acclamation. The decision of the meeting was supreme and final. "Whenever a matter is discussed," says Schoemann in "Antiquities of Greece, "which requires the participation of the people for its execution, Homer does not indicate any means by which the people could be forced to it against their will." It is evident that at a time when every ablebodied member of the tribe was a warrior, there existed as yet no public power apart from the people that might have been used against them. The primordial democracy was still in full force, and by this

THE GRECIAN GENS

standard the influence and position of the council and of the basileus must be judged.

3. The military chief (basileus). Marx makes the following comment: "The European scientists, mostly born servants of princes, represent the basileus as a monarch in the modern sense. The Yankee republican Morgan objects to this. Very ironically but truthfully he says of the oily Gladstone and his "Juventus Mundi': 'Mr. Gladstone, who presents to his readers the Grecian chiefs of the heroic age as kings and princes, with the superadded qualities of gentlemen, is forced to admit that, on the whole we seem to have the custom or law of primogeniture sufficiently, but not oversharply defined.' As a matter of fact, Mr. Gladstone himself must have perceived that a primogeniture resting on a clause of 'sufficient but not oversharp' definition is as bad as none at all."

We saw how the law of heredity was applied to the offices of sachems and chiefs among the Iroquois and other Indians. All offices were subject to the vote of the gentiles and for this reason hereditary in the gens. A vacancy was filled preferably by the next gentile relative—the brother or the sister's son—unless good reasons existed for passing him. That in Greece, under paternal law, the office of basileus was generally transmitted to the son or one of the sons, indicates only that the probability of succession by public election was in favor of the sons. It implies by no means a legal succession without a vote of the people. We here perceive simply the first rudiments of segregated families of aristocrats among Iroquois and Greeks, which led to a hereditary leadership or monarchy in Greece. Hence the facts are in favor of the opinion that among Greeks the basileus was either elected by the people or at last was subject to the indorsement of their appointed organs, the council or agora, as was the case with the Roman king (rex).

THE ORIGIN OF THE FAMILY

In the Iliad the ruler of men, Agamemnon, does not appear as the supreme king of the Greeks, but as general in chief of a federal army besieging a city. And when dissensions had broken out among the Greeks, it is this quality which Odysseus points out in a famous passage: "Evil is the rule of the many; let one be the ruler, one the chief" (to which the popular verse about the scepter was added later on). Odysseus does not lecture on the form of government, but demands obedience to the general in chief.

Considering that the Greeks before Troy appear only in the character of an army, the proceedings of the agora are sufficiently democratic. In referring to presents, that is the division of the spoils, Achilles always leaves the division, not to Agamemnon or some other basileus, but to the "sons of the Achaeans," the people. The attributes, descendant of Zeus, bred by Zeus, do not prove anything, because every gens is descended from some god—the gens of the leader of the tribe from a "prominent" god, in this case Zeus. Even those who are without personal freedom, as the swineherd Eumaeos and others, are "divine" (dioi or theioi), even in the Odyssey, which belongs to a much later period than the Iliad. In the same Odyssey, the name of "heros" is given to the herald Mulios as well as to the blind bard Demodokos. In short, the word "basileia," with which the Greek writers designate the so-called monarchy of Homer (because the military leadership is its distinguishing mark, by the side of which the council and the agora are existing), means simply—military democracy (Marx).

The basileus had also sacerdotal and judiciary functions beside those of a military leader. The judiciary functions are not clearly defined, but the functions of priesthood are due to his position of chief representative of the tribe or of the league of tribes. There is never any mention of civil, administrative functions.

THE GRECIAN GENS

But it seems that he was ex-officio a member of the council. The translation of basileus by king is etymologically quite correct, because king (Kuning) is derived from Kuni, Künne, and signifies chief of a gens. But the modern meaning of the word king in no way designates the functions of the Grecian basileus. Thucydides expressly refers to the old basileia as patrikê, that is "derived from the gens," and states that it had well defined functions. And Aristotle says that the basileia of heroic times was a leadership of free men and that the basileus was a military chief, a judge and a high priest. Hence the basileus had no governmental power in a modern sense.*

In the Grecian constitution of heroic times, then, we still find the old gentilism fully alive, but we also perceive the beginnings of the elements that undermine it; paternal law and inheritance of property by the father's children, favoring accumulation of wealth in the family and giving to the latter a power apart from the gens; influence of the difference of wealth on the constitution by the formation of the first rudiments of hereditary nobility and monarchy, slavery, first limited to prisoners of war, but already paving the way to the enslavement of tribal and gentile associates; degeneration of the old feuds between tribes a regular mode of existing by systematic plundering on

---

Author's note.
*Just as the Grecian basileus, so the Aztec military chief was misrepresented as a modern prince. Morgan was the first to submit to historical criticism the reports of the Spaniards who first misapprehended and exaggerated, and later on consciously misrepresented the functions of this office. He showed that the Mexicans were in the middle stage of barbarism, but on a higher plane than the New Mexican Pueblo Indians, and that their constitution, so far as the garbled accounts show, corresponded to this stage: a league of three tribes which had made a number of others tributary and was administered by a federal council and a federal chief of war, whom the Spaniards construed into an "emperor."

THE ORIGIN OF THE FAMILY

land and sea for the purpose of acquiring cattle, slaves, and treasures. In short, wealth is praised and respected as the highest treasure, and the old gentile institutions are abused in order to justify the forcible robbery of wealth. Only one thing was missing: an institution that not only secured the newly acquired property of private individuals against the communistic traditions of the gens, that not only declared as sacred the formerly so despised private property and represented the protection of this sacred property as the highest purpose of human society, but that also stamped the gradually developing new forms of acquiring property, of constantly increasing wealth, with the universal sanction of society. An institution that lent the character of perpetuity not only to the newly rising division into classes, but also to the right of the possessing classes to exploit and rule the non-possessing classes.

And this institution was found. The state arose.

CHAPTER V.

ORIGIN OF THE ATTIC STATE.

How the state gradually developed by partly transforming the organs of the gentile constitution, partly replacing them by new organs and finally installing real state authorities; how the place of the nation in arms defending itself through its gentes, phratries and tribes, was taken by an armed public power of coërcion in the hands of these authorities and available against the mass of the people; nowhere can we observe the first act of this drama so well as in ancient Athens. The essential stages of the various transformations are outlined by Morgan, but the analysis of the economic causes producing them is largely added by myself.

In the heroic period, the four tribes of the Athenians were still installed in separate parts of Attica. Even the twelve phratries composing them seem to have had separate seats in the twelve different towns of Cecrops. The constitution was in harmony with the period: a public meeting (agorâ), a council (bûlê) and a basileus.

As far back as we can trace written history we find the land divided up and in the possession of private individuals. For during the last period of the higher stage of barbarism the production of commodities and the resulting trade had well advanced. Grain, wine and oil were staple articles. The sea trade on the Aegean Sea drifted more and more out of the hands of the Phoenicians into those of the Athenians. By the purchase and sale of land, by continued division of labor between agriculture and industry, trade

THE ORIGIN OF THE FAMILY

and navigation, the members of gentes, phratries and tribes very soon intermingled. The districts of the phratry and the tribe received inhabitants who did not belong to these bodies and, therefore, were strangers in their own homes, although they were countrymen. For during times of peace, every phratry and every tribe administered its own affairs without consulting the council of Athens or the basileus. But inhabitants not belonging to the phratry or the tribe could not take part in the administration of these bodies.

Thus the well-regulated functions of the gentile organs became so disarranged that relief was already needed during the heroic period. A constitution attributed to Theseus was introduced. The main feature of this change was the institution of a central administration in Athens. A part of the affairs that had so long been conducted autonomously by the tribes was declared collective business and transferred to a general council in Athens. This step of the Athenians went farther than any ever taken by the nations of America. For the simple federation of autonomous tribes was now replaced by the conglomeration of all tribes into one single body. The next result was a common Athenian law, standing above the legal traditions of the tribes and gentes. It bestowed on the citizens of Athens certain privileges and legal protection, even in a territory that did not belong to their tribe. This meant another blow to the gentile constitution; for it opened the way to the admission of citizens who were not members of any Attic tribe and stood entirely outside of the Athenian gentile constitution.

A second institution attributed to Theseus was the division of the entire nation into three classes regardless of the gentes, phratries and tribes: eupatrides or nobles, geomoroi or farmers, and demiurgoi or trades-

ORIGIN OF THE ATTIC STATE

men. The exclusive privilege of the nobles to fill the offices was included in this innovation. Apart from this privilege the new division remained ineffective, as it did not create any legal distinctions between the classes. But it is important, because it shows us the new social elements that had developed in secret. It shows that the habitual holding of gentile offices by certain families had already developed into a practically uncontested privilege; that these families, already powerful through their wealth, began to combine outside of their gentes into a privileged class; and that the just arising state sanctioned this assumption. It shows furthermore that the division of labor between farmers and tradesmen had grown strong enough to contest the supremacy of the old gentile and tribal division of society. And finally it proclaims the irreconcilable opposition of gentile society to the state. The first attempt to form a state broke up the gentes by dividing their members against one another and opposing a privileged class to a class of disowned belonging to two different branches of production.

The ensuing political history of Athens up to the time of Solon is only incompletely known. The office of basileus became obsolete. Archons elected from the ranks of the nobility occupied the leading position in the state. The power of the nobility increased continually, until it became unbearable about the year 600 before Christ. The principal means for stifling the liberty of the people were—money and usury. The main seat of the nobility was in and around Athens. There the sea trade and now and then a little convenient piracy enriched them and concentrated the money into their hands. From this point the gradually arising money power penetrated like corrugating acid into the traditional modes of rural existence founded on natural economy. The gentile constitution is absolutely irreconcilable with money rule. The

THE ORIGIN OF THE FAMILY

ruin of the Attic farmers coincided with the loosening of the old gentile bonds that protected them. The debtor's receipt and the pawning of the property—for the mortgage was also invented by the Athenians—cared neither for the gens nor for the phratry. But the old gentile constitution knew nothing of money, advance and debt. Hence the ever more virulently spreading money rule of the nobility developed a new legal custom, securing the creditor against the debtor and sanctioning the exploitation of the small farmer by the wealthy. All the rural districts of Attica were crowded with mortgage columns bearing the legend that the lot on which they stood was mortgaged to such and such for so much. The fields that were not so designated had for the most part been sold on account of overdue mortgages or interest and transferred to the aristocratic usurers. The farmer could thank his stars, if he was granted permission to live as a tenant on one-sixth of the product of his labor and to pay five-sixths to his new master in the form of rent. Worse still, if the sale of the lot did not bring sufficient returns to cover the debt, or if such a debt had been contracted without a lien, then the debtor had to sell his children into slavery abroad in order to satisfy the claim of the creditor. The sale of the children by the father—that was the first fruit of paternal law and monogamy! And if that did not satisfy the bloodsuckers, they could sell the debtor himself into slavery. Such was the pleasant dawn of civilization among the people of Attica.

Formerly, while the condition of the people was in keeping with gentile traditions, a similar downfall would have been impossible. But here it had come about, nobody knew how. Let us return for a moment to the Iroquois. The state of things that had imposed itself on the Athenians almost without their doing, so to say, and assuredly against their will, was incon-

ORIGIN OF THE ATTIC STATE

ceivable among the Indians. There the ever unchanging mode of production could at no time generate such conflicts as a distinction between rich and poor, exploiters and exploited, caused by external conditions. The Iroquois were far from controlling the forces of nature, but within the limits drawn for them by nature they dominated their own production. Apart from a failure of the crops in their little gardens, the exhaustion of the fish supply in their lakes and rivers or of the game stock in their forests, they always knew what would be the outcome of their mode of gaining a living. A more or less abundant supply of food, that would come of it. But the outcome could never be any unpremeditated social upheavals, breaking of gentile bonds or division of the gentiles against one another by conflicting class interests. Production was carried on in the most limited manner; but—the producers controlled their own product. This immense advantage of barbarian production was lost in the transition to civilization. To win it back on the basis of man's present gigantic control of nature and of the free association rendered possible by it, that will be the task of the next generations.

Not so among the Greeks. The advent of private property in herds of cattle and articles of luxury led to an exchange between individuals, to a transformation of products into commodities. Here is the root of the entire revolution that followed. When the producers did no longer consume their own product, but released their hold of it in exchange for another's product, then they lost the control of it. They did not know any more what became of it. There was a possibility that the product might be turned against the producers for the purpose of exploiting and oppressing them. No society can, therefore, retain for any length of time the control of its own produc-

THE ORIGIN OF THE FAMILY

tion and of the social effects of the mode of production, unless it abolishes exchange between individuals.

How rapidly after the establishment of individual exchange and after the transformation of products into commodities the product manifests its rule over the producer, the Athenians were soon to learn. Along with the production of marketable commodities came the tilling of the soil by individual cultivators for their own account, soon followed by individual ownership of the land. Along came also the money, that general commodity for which all others could be exchanged. But when men invented money they little suspected that they were creating a new social power, that one universal power before which the whole of society must bow down. It was this new power, suddenly sprung into existence without the forethought and intention of its own creators, that vented its rule on the Athenians with the full brutality of youth.

What was to be done? The old gentile organization had not only proved impotent against the triumphant march of money; it was also absolutely incapable of containing within its confines any such thing as money, creditors, debtors and forcible collection of debts. But the new social power was upon them and neither pious wishes nor a longing for the return of the good old times could drive money and usury from the face of the earth. Moreover, gentile constitution had suffered a number of minor defeats. The indiscriminate mingling of the gentiles and phrators in the whole of Attica, and especially in Athens, had assumed larger proportions from generation to generation. Still even now a citizen of Athens was not allowed to sell his residence outside of his gens, although he could do so with plots of land. The division of labor between the different branches of production—agriculture, trades, numberless specialties within the trades, com

ORIGIN OF THE ATTIC STATE

merce, navigation, etc.—had developed more fully with the progress of industry and traffic. The population was now divided according to occupations into rather well defined groups, everyone of which had separate interests not guarded by the gens or phratry and therefore necessitating the creation of new offices The number of slaves had increased considerably and must have surpassed by far that of the free Athenians even at this early stage. Gentile society originally knew no slavery and was, therefore, ignorant of any means to hold this mass of bondsmen in check. And finally, commerce had attracted a great many strangers who settled in Athens for the sake of the easier living it afforded. According to the old constitution, the strangers had neither civil rights nor the protection of the law. Though tacitly admitted by tradition, they remained a disturbing and foreign element.

In short, gentile constitution approached its doom. Society was daily growing more and more beyond it. It was powerless to stop or allay even the most distressing evils that had grown under its very eyes. But in the meantime the state had secretly developed. The new groups formed by division of labor, first between city and country, then between the various branches of city industry, had created new organs for the care of their interests. Public offices of every description had been instituted. And above all the young state needed its own fighting forces. Among the seafaring Athenians this had to be at first only a navy, for occasional short expeditions and the protection of the merchant vessels. At some uncertain time before Solon, the naukrariai were instituted, little territorial districts, twelve in each tribe. Every naukraria had to furnish, equip and man a war vessel and to detail two horsemen. This arrangement was a twofold attack on the gentile constitution. In the first place it created

THE ORIGIN OF THE FAMILY

a public power of coërcion that did no longer absolutely coincide with the entirety of the armed nation. In the second place it was the first division of the people for public purposes, not by groups of kinship, but by local residence. We shall soon see what that signified.

As the gentile constitution could not come to the assistance of the exploited people, they could look only to the rising state. And the state brought help in the form of the constitution of Solon. At the same time it added to its own strength at the expense of the old constitution. Solon opened the series of so-called political revolutions by an infringement on private property. We pass over the means by which this reform was accomplished in the year 594 B. C. or thereabout. Ever since, all revolutions have been revolutions for the protection of one kind of property against another kind of property. They cannot protect one kind without violating another. In the great French revolution the feudal property was sacrificed for the sake of saving bourgeois property. In Solon's revolution, the property of the creditors had to make concessions to the property of the debtors. The debts were simply declared illegal. We are not acquainted with the accurate details, but Solon boasts in his poëms that he removed the mortgage columns from the indented lots and enabled all who had fled or been sold abroad for debts to return home. This was only feasible by an open violation of private property. And indeed, all so-called political revolutions were started for the protection of one kind of property by the confiscation, also called theft, of another kind of property. It is absolutely true that for more than 2,500 years private property could only be protected by the violation of private property.

But now a way had to be found to avoid the return of such an enslavement of the free Athenians. This

ORIGIN OF THE ATTIC STATE

was first attempted by general measures, e. g., the prohibition of contracts giving the person of the debtor in lien. Furthermore a maximum limit was fixed for the amount of land any one individual could own, in order to keep the craving of the nobility for the land of the farmers within reasonable bounds. Constitutional amendments were next in order. The following deserve special consideration:

The council was increased to four hundred members, one hundred from each tribe. Here, then, the tribe still served as a basis. But this was the only remnant of the old constitution that was transferred to the new body politic. For otherwise Solon divided the citizens into four classes according to their property in land and its yield. Five hundred, three hundred and one hundred and fifty medimnoi of grain (1 medimnos equals 1.16 bushels) were the minimum yields of the first three classes. Whoever had less land or none at all belonged to the fourth class. Only members of the first three classes could hold office; the highest offices were filled by the first class. The fourth class had only the right to speak and vote in the public council. But here all officials were elected, here they had to give account, here all the laws were made, and here the fourth class was in the majority. The aristocratic privileges were partly renewed in the form of privileges of wealth, but the people retained the decisive power. The four classes also formed the basis for the reorganization of the fighting forces. The first two classes furnished the horsemen; the third had to serve as heavy infantry; the fourth was employed as light unarmored infantry and had to man the navy. Probably the last class also received wages in this case.

An entirely new element is thus introduced into the constitution: private property. The rights and duties of the citizens are graduated according to their property in land. Wherever the classification by property

THE ORIGIN OF THE FAMILY

gains ground, there the old groups of blood relationship give way. Gentile constitution has suffered another defeat.

However, the gradation of political rights according to private property was not one of those institutions without which a state cannot exist. It may have been ever so important in the constitutional development of some states. Still a good many others, and the most completely developed at that, had no need of it. Even in Athens it played only a passing role. Since the time of Aristides, all offices were open to all the citizens.

During the next eighty years the Athenian society gradually drifted into the course on which it further developed in the following centuries. The outrageous land speculation of the time before Solon had been fettered, likewise the excessive concentration of property in land. Commerce, trades and artisan handicrafts, which were carried on in an ever larger scale as slave labor increased, became the ruling factors in gaining a living. Public enlightenment advanced. Instead of exploiting their own fellow citizens in the old brutal style, the Athenians now exploited mainly the slaves and the customers outside. Movable property, wealth in money, slaves and ships, increased more and more. But instead of being a simple means for the purchase of land, as in the old stupid times, it had now become an end in itself. The new class of industrial and commercial owners of wealth now waged a victorious competition against the old nobility. The remnants of the old gentile constitution lost their last hold. The gentes, phratries and tribes, the members of which now were dispersed all over Attica and completely intermixed, had thus become unavailable as political groups. A great many citizens of Athens did not belong to any gens. They were immigrants who had been adopted into citizenship, but not

ORIGIN OF THE ATTIC STATE

into any of the old groups of kinship. Besides, there was a steadily increasing number of foreign immigrants who were only protected by traditional sufferance.

Meanwhile the struggles of the parties proceeded. The nobility tried to regain their former privileges and for a short time recovered their supremacy, until the revolution of Kleisthenes (509 B. C.) brought their final downfall and completed the ruin of gentile law.

In his new constitution, Kleisthenes ignored the four old tribes founded on the gentes and phraties. Their place was taken by an entirely new organization based on the recently attempted division of the citizens into naukrariai according to residence. No longer was membership in a group of kindred the dominant fact, but simply local residence. Not the nation, but the territory was now divided; the inhabitants became mere political fixtures of the territory.

The whole of Attica was divided into one hundred communal districts, so-called demoi, every one of which was autonomous. The citizens living in a demos (demotoi) elected their official head (demarchos), treasurer and thirty judges with jurisdiction in minor cases. They also received their own temple and divine guardian or heros, whose priest they elected. The control of the demos was in the hands of the council of demotoi. This is, as Morgan correctly remarks, the prototype of the autonomous American township. The modern state in its highest development ended in the same unit with which the rising state began its career in Athens.

Ten of these units (demoi) formed a tribe, which, however, was now designated as local tribe in order to distinguish it from the old sex tribe. The local tribe was not only an autonomous political, but also a military group. It elected the phylarchos or tribal head who commanded the horsemen, the taxiarchos commanding the infantry and the strategic leader, who was in command of the entire contingent raised in the tribal territory by conscription. The local tribe furthermore furnished, equipped and fully manned five war vessels. It was designated by the name of the Attic hero who was its guardian deity. It elected fifty councilmen into the council of Athens.

Thus we arrive at the Athenian state, governed by a council of five hundred elected by and representing the ten tribes and subject to the vote of the public meeting, where every citizen could enter and vote. Archons and other officials attended to the different departments of administration and justice.

By this new constitution and by the admission of a large number of aliens, partly freed slaves, partly immigrants, the organs of gentile constitution were displaced in public affairs. They became mere private and religious clubs. But their moral influence, the traditional conceptions and views of the old gentile period, survived for a long time and expired only gradually. This was evident in another state institution.

We have seen that an essential mark of the state consists in a public power of coërcion divorced from the mass of the people. Athens possessed at that time only a militia and a navy equipped and manned directly by the people. These afforded protection against external enemies and held the slaves in check, who at that time already made up the large majority of the population. For the citizens, this coërcive power at first only existed in the shape of the police, which is as old as the state. The innocent Frenchmen of the 18th century, therefore, had the habit of speaking not of civilized, but of policed nations (nations policées). The Athenians, then, provided for a police in their new state, a veritable "force" of bowmen on foot

ORIGIN OF THE ATTIC STATE

and horseback. This police force consisted—of slaves. The free Athenian regarded this police duty as so degrading that he preferred being arrested by an armed slave rather than lending himself to such an ignominious service. That was still a sign of the old gentile spirit. The state could not exist without a police, but as yet it was too young and did not command sufficient moral respect to give prestige to an occupation that necessarily appeared ignominious to the old gentiles.

How well this state, now completed in its main outlines, suited the social condition of the Athenians was apparent by the rapid growth of wealth, commerce and industry. The distinction of classes on which the social and political institutions are resting was no longer between nobility and common people, but between slaves and freemen, aliens and citizens. At the time of the greatest prosperity the whole number of free Athenian citizens, women and children included, amounted to about 90,000; the slaves of both sexes numbered 365,000 and the aliens—foreigners and freed slaves—45,000. Per capita of each adult citizen there were, therefore, at least eighteen slaves and more than two aliens. The great number of slaves is explained by the fact that many of them worked together in large factories under supervision. The development of commerce and industry brought about an accumulation and concentration of wealth in a few hands. The mass of the free citizens were impoverished and had to face the choice of either competing with their own labor against slave labor, which was considered ignoble and vile, besides promising little success, or to be ruined. Under the prevailing circumstances they necessarily chose the latter course and being in the majority they ruined the whole Attic state. Not democracy caused the downfall of Athens, as the European glorifiers of princes and lickspittle

THE ORIGIN OF THE FAMILY

schoolmasters would have us believe, but slavery ostracizing the labor of the free citizen.

The origin of the state among the Athenians presents a very typical form of state organization. For it took place without any marring external interference or internal obstruction—the usurpation of Pisistratos left no trace of its short duration. It shows the direct rise of a highly developed form of a state, the democratic republic, out of gentile society. And finally, we are sufficiently acquainted with all the essential details of the process.

CHAPTER VI.

GENS AND STATE IN ROME.

The legend of the foundation of Rome sets forth that the first colonization was undertaken by a number of Latin gentes (one hundred, so the legend says) united into one tribe. A Sabellian tribe (also said to consist of one hundred gentes) soon followed, and finally a third tribe of various elements, but again numbering one hundred gentes, joined them. The whole tale reveals at the first glance that little more than the gens was borrowed from reality, and that the gens itself was in certain cases only an offshoot of an old mother gens still existing at home. The tribes bear the mark of artificial composition on their foreheads; still they were made up of kindred elements and after the model of the old spontaneous, not artificial tribe. At the same time it is not impossible that a genuine old tribe formed the nucleus of every one of these three tribes. The connecting link, the phratry, contained ten gentes and was called curia. Hence there were thirty curiae.

The Roman gens is recognized as an institution identical with the Grecian gens. The Grecian gens being a continuation of the same social unit, the primordial form of which we found among the American Indians, the same holds naturally good of the Roman gens, and we can be more concise in its treatment.

At least during the most ancient times of the city, the Roman gens had the following constitution:

1. Mutual right of inheritance for gentiles; the

THE ORIGIN OF THE FAMILY

wealth remained in the gens. Paternal law being already in force in the Roman the same as in the Grecian gens, the offspring of female lineage were excluded. According to the law of the twelve tablets, the oldest written law of Rome known to us, the natural children had the first title to the estate; in case no natural children existed, the agnati (kin of male lineage) took their place; and last in line came the gentiles. In all cases the property remained in the gens. Here we observe the gradual introduction of new legal provisions, caused by increased wealth and monogamy, into the gentile practice. The originally equal right of inheritance of the gentiles was first limited in practice to the agnati, no doubt at a very remote date, and afterwards to the natural children and their offspring of male lineage. Of course this appears in the reverse order on the twelve tablets.

2. Possession of a common burial ground. The patrician gens Claudia, on immigrating into Rome from Regilli, was assigned to a separate lot of land and received its own burial ground in the city. As late as the time of Augustus, the head of Varus, who had been killed in the Teutoburger Wald, was brought to Rome and interred in the gentilitius tumulus; hence his gens (Quinctilia) still had its own tomb.

3. Common religious rites. These are well-known under the name of sacra gentilitia.

4. Obligation not to intermarry in the gens. It seems that this was never a written law in Rome, but the custom remained. Among the innumerable names of Roman couples preserved for us there is not a single case, where husband and wife had the same gentile name. The law of inheritance proves the same rule. By marrying, a woman loses her agnatic privileges, discards her gens, and neither she nor her children have any title to her father's estate nor to that of his brothers, because otherwise the gens of her father

GENS AND STATE IN ROME

would lose his property. This rule has a meaning only then when the woman is not permitted to marry a gentile.

5. A common piece of land. In primeval days this was always obtained when the tribal territory was first divided. Among the Latin tribes we find the land partly in the possession of the tribe, partly of the gens, and partly of the households that could hardly represent single families at such an early date. Romulus is credited with being the first to assign land to single individuals, about 2.47 acres (two jugera) per head. But later on we still find some land in the hands of the gentes, not to mention the state land, around which turns the whole internal history of the republic.

6. Duty of the gentiles to mutually protect and assist one another. Written history records only remnants of this law. The Roman state from the outset manifested such superior power, that the duty of protection against injury devolved upon it. When Appius Claudius was arrested, his whole gens, including his personal enemies, dressed in mourning. At the time of the second Punic war the gentes united for the purpose of ransoming their captured gentiles. The senate vetoed this.

7. Right to bear the gentile name. This was in force until the time of the emperors. Freed slaves were permitted to assume the gentile name of their former master, but this did not bestow any gentile rights on them.

8. Right of adopting strangers into the gens. This was done by adoption into the family (the same as among the Indians) which brought with it the adoption into the gens.

9. The right to elect and depose chiefs is not mentioned anywhere. But inasmuch as during the first years of Rome's existence all offices were filled by election or nomination, from the king downward, and

THE ORIGIN OF THE FAMILY

as the curiae elected also their own priests, we are justified in assuming the same in regard to gentile chiefs (principes)—no matter how well established the rule of choosing the candidates from the same family have been.

Such were the constitutional rights of a Roman gens. With the exception of the completed transition to paternal law, they are the true image of the rights and duties of an Iroquois gens. Here, also, "the Iroquois is still plainly visible."

How confused the ideas of our historians, even the most prominent of them, are when it comes to a discussion of the Roman gens, is shown by the following example: In Mommsen's treatise on the Roman family names of the Republican and Augustinian era (Römische Forschungen, Berlin, 1864, Vol. I.) he writes: "The gentile name was not only borne by all male gentiles including all adopted and wards, except, of course, the slaves, but also by the women. . . . The tribe (so Mommsen translates gens) is a common organization resulting from a common—actual, assumed or even invented—ancestor and united by common rites, burial grounds and customs of inheritance. All free individuals, hence women also, may and must claim membership in them. But the definition of the gentile name of the married women offers some difficulty. This is indeed obviated, as long as women were not permitted to marry any one but their gentiles. And we have proofs that for a long time the women found it much more difficult to marry outside than inside of the gens. This right of marrying outside, the gentis enuptio, was still bestowed as a personal privilege and reward during the sixth century. . . . But wherever such outside marriages occurred in primeval times, the woman must have been transferred to the tribe of her husband. Nothing is more certain than that by the old religious marriage woman

GENS AND STATE IN ROME

was completely adopted into the legal and sacramental group of her husband and divorced from her own. Who does not know that the married woman releases her active and passive right of inheritance in favor of her gentiles, but enters the legal group of her husband, her children and his gentiles? And if her husband adopts her as his child into his family, how can she remain separated from his gens?" (Pages 9-11.)

Here Mommsen asserts that the Roman women belonging to a certain gens were originally free to marry only within their gens; the Roman gens, according to him, was therefore endogamous, not exogamous. This opinion which contradicts the evidence of all other nations, is principally, if not exclusively, founded on a single much disputed passage of Livy (Book xxxix, c. 19). According to this passage, the senate decreed in the year 568 of the city, i. e., 186 B. C., (uti Feceniae Hispallae datio, deminutio, gentis enuptio, tutoris optio idem esset quasi ei vir testamento dedisset; utique ei ingenuo nubere liceret, neu quid ei qui eam duxisset, ob id fraudi ignominiaeve esset)—that Fecenia Hispalla shall have the right to dispose of her property, to diminish it, to marry outside of the gens, to choose a guardian, just as if her (late) husband ha conferred this right on her by testament; that sh shall be permitted to marry a freeman and that for the man who marries her this shall not constitute a misdemeanor or a shame.

Without a doubt Fecenia, a freed slave, here obtains permission to marry outside of the gens. And equally doubtless the husband here has the right to confer on his wife by testament the right to marry outside of the gens after his death. But outside of which gens?

If a woman had to intermarry in the gens, as Mommsen assumes, then she remained in this gens after her marriage. But in the first place, this assertion of an endogamous gens must be proven. And in the second

THE ORIGIN OF THE FAMILY

place, if the women had to intermarry in the gens, then the men had to do the same, otherwise there could be no marriage. Then we arrive at the conclusion that the man could bequeath a right to his wife, which he did not have for himself. This is a legal impossibility. Mommsen feels this very well, and hence he supposes: "The marriage outside of the gens most probably required not only the consent of the testator, but of all gentiles." (Page 10, footnote.) This is not only a very daring assertion, but contradicts also the clear wording of the passage. The senate gives her this right as a proxy of her husband; they expressly give her no more and no less than her husband could have given her, but what they do give is an absolute right, independent of all limitations, so that, if she should make use of it, her new husband shall not suffer in consequence. The senate even instructs the present and future consuls and praetors to see that no inconvenience arise to her from the use of this right. Mommsen's supposition is therefore absolutely inadmissible.

Then again: suppose a woman married a man from another gens, but remained in her own gens. According to the passage quoted above, her husband would then have had the right to permit his wife to marry outside of her own gens. That is, he would have had the right to make provisions in regard to the affairs of a gens to which he did not belong at all. The thing is so utterly unreasonable that we need not lose any words about it.

Nothing remains but to assume that the woman in her first marriage wedded a man from another gens and thereby became a member of her husband's gens. Mommsen admits this for such cases. Then the whole matter at once explains itself. The women, torn away from her old gens by her marriage and adopted into the gentile group of her husband, occupies a peculiar

GENS AND STATE IN ROME

position in the new gens. She is now a gentile, but not a kin by blood. The manner of her entrance from the outset excludes all prohibition of intermarrying in the gens, into which she has come by marriage. She is adopted into the family relations of the gens and inherits some of the property of her husband when he dies, the property of a gentile. What is more natural than that this property should remain in the gens and that she should be obliged to marry a gentile of her husband and no other? If, however, an exception is to be made, who is so well entitled to authorize her as her first husband who bequeathed his property to her? At the moment when he bequeathes on her a part of his property and simultaneously gives her permission to transfer this property by marriage or as a result of marriage to a strange gens, he still is the owner of this property, hence he literally disposes of his personal property. As for the woman and her relation to the gens of her husband, it is he who by an act of his own free will—the marriage—introduced her into his gens. Therefore it seems quite natural that he should be the proper person to authorize her to leave this gens by another marriage. In short, the matter appears simple and obvious, as soon as we discard the absurd conception of an endogamous Roman gens and accept Morgan's originally exogamous gens.

There is still another view which has probably found the greatest number of advocates. According to them the passage in Livy only means "that freed slave girls (libertae) cannot without special permission, e gente enubere (marry outside of the gens) or undertake any of the steps which, together with capitis deminutio minima* (the loss of family rights) would lead to a

---
Translator's note.
*The term caput received the meaning of legal right of a person from the legal status of the head of a family.

THE ORIGIN OF THE FAMILY

transfer of the liberta to another gens." (Lange, Römische Alterthümer, Berlin, 1856, I, p. 185, where our passage from Livy is explained by a reference to Huschke.) If this view is correct, then the passage proves still less for the relations of free Roman women, and there is so much less ground for speaking of their obligation to intermarry in the gens.

The expression enuptio gentis (marriage outside of the gens) occurs only in this single passage and is not found anywhere else in the entire Roman literature. The word enubere (to marry outside) is found only three times likewise in Livy, and not in reference to the gens. The phantastic idea that Roman women had to intermarry in the gens owes its existence only to this single passage. But it cannot be maintained. For either the passage refers to special restrictions for freed slave women, in which case it proves nothing for free women (ingenuae). Or it applies also to free women, in which case it rather proves that the women as a rule married outside of the gens and were transferred by their marriage to their husbands' gens. This would be a point for Morgan against Mommsen.

Almost three hundred years after the foundation of Rome the gentile bonds were still so strong that a patrician gens, the Fabians, could obtain permission from the senate to undertake all by itself a war expedition against the neighboring town of Veii. Three hundred and six Fabians are said to have marched

. . . . . Legal science extended the meaning of the term so that it related not alone to slaves, but also to minors and women. This legal right, so conceived, could be curtailed in three ways: Capitis deminutio maxima was the loss of the status libertatis (personal liberty), which included the loss of the status civitatis and familiae (civil and family rights); the capitis deminutio minor or media was the loss of the status civitatis (civil rights), including the loss of the status familiae (family rights); the capitis deminutio minima was the loss of the status familiae (family rights). Lange, Romische Alterthumer, Berlin, 1876, Vol. I., p. 204.

GENS AND STATE IN ROME

and to have been killed from ambush. Only one boy was left behind to propagate the gens.

Ten gentes, we said, formed a phratry, named curia. It was endowed with more important functions than the Grecian phratry. Every curia had its own religious rites, sacred possessions and priests. The priests of one curia in a body formed one of the Roman clerical collegiums. Ten curiae formed a tribe which probably had originally its own elected chief—leader in war and high priest—like the rest of the Latin tribes. The three tribes together formed the populus Romanus, the Roman people.

Hence nobody could belong to the Roman people, unless he was a member of a Roman gens, and thus a member of a curia and tribe. The first constitution of the Roman people was as follows. Public affairs were conducted by the Senate composed, as Niebuhr was the first to state correctly, of the chiefs of the three hundred gentes. Because they were the elders of the gentes they were called patres, fathers, and as a body senatus, council of elders, from senex, old. Here also the customary choice of men from the same family of the gens brought to life the first hereditary nobility. These families were called patricians and claimed the exclusive right to the seats in the senate and to all other offices. The fact that in the course of time the people admitted this claim so that it became an actual privilege is confirmed by the legendary report that Romulus bestowed the rank of patrician and its privileges on the first senators. The senate, like the Athenian boulê, had to make the final decision in many affairs and to undertake the preliminary discussion of more important matters, especially of new laws. These were settled by the public meeting, the so-called comitia curiata (assembly of curiae.) The people met in curiae, probably grouped by gentes, and every one of the thirty curiae had one vote. The

THE ORIGIN OF THE FAMILY

assembly of curiae adopted or rejected all laws, elected all higher officials including the rex (so-called king), declared war (but the senate concluded peace), and decided as a supreme court, on appeal, all cases involving capital punishment of Roman citizens. By the side of the senate and the public meeting stood the rex, corresponding to the Grecian basileus, and by no means such an almost absolute king as Mommsen would have it.* The rex was also a military leader, a high priest and a chairman of certain courts. He had no other functions, nor any power over life, liberty and property of the citizens, except such as resulted from his disciplinary power as military leader or from his executive power as president of a court. The office of rex was not hereditary. On the contrary, he was elected, probably on the suggestion of his predecessor, by the assembly of curiae and then solemnly invested by a second assembly. That he could also be deposed is proved by the fate of Tarquinius Superbus.

As the Greeks at the time of the heroes, so the Romans at the time of the so-called kings lived in a military democracy based on and developed from a constitution of gentes, phratries and tribes. What though the curiae and tribes were partly artificial formations, they were moulded after the genuine and spontaneous models of a society from which they originated and that still surrounded them on all sides.

Author's note.

*The Latin rex is equivalent to the Celtic-Irish righ (tribal chief) and the Gothic reiks. That this, like the German Furst, English first and Danish forste, originally signified gentile or tribal chief is evident from the fact that the Goths in the fourth century already had a special term for the king of later times, the military chief of a whole nation, viz., thiudans. In Ulfila's translation of the Bible Artaxerxes and Herod are never called reiks, but thiudans, and the empire of the emperor Tiberius not reiki, but thiudinassus. In the name of the Gothic thiudans, or king as we inaccurately translate, Thiudareiks (Theodoric, German Dietrich), both names flow together.

GENS AND STATE IN ROME

And though the sturdy patrician nobility had already gained ground, though the reges attempted gradually to enlarge the scope of their functions—all this does not change the elementary and fundamental character of the constitution, and this alone is essential.

Meantime the population of the city of Rome and of the Roman territory, enlarged by conquest, increased partly by immigration, partly through the inhabitants of the annexed districts, Latins most of them. All these new members of the state (we disregard here the clients) stood outside of the old gentes, curiae and tribes and so did not form a part of the populus Romanus, the Roman people proper. They were personally free, could own land, had to pay taxes and were subject to military service. But they were not eligible to office and could neither take part in the assembly of curiae nor in the distribution of conquered state lands. They made up the mass of people excluded from all public rights, the plebs. By their continually growing numbers, their military training and armament they became a threat for the old populus who now closed their ranks hermetically against all new elements. The land seems to have been about evenly divided between populus and plebs, while the mercantile and industrial wealth, though as yet not very considerable, may have been mainly in the hands of the plebs.

In view of the utter darkness that enwraps the whole legendary origin of Rome's historical beginning —a darkness that was rendered still more intense by the rationalistic and overofficious interpretations and reports of the juristically trained authors that wrote on the subject—it is impossible to make any definite statements about the time, the course and the motive of the revolution that put an end to the old gentile constitution. We are certain only that the causes

THE ORIGIN OF THE FAMILY

arose out of the fights between the plebs and the populus.

The new constitution, attributed to rex Servius Tullius and following the Grecian model, more especially that of Solon, created a new public assembly including or excluding all the members of populus and plebs according to whether they rendered military service or not. The whole population, subject to enlistment, was divided into six classes according to wealth. The lowest limitis in the five highest classes were: I., 100,000 ass; II., 75,000; III., 50,000; IV., 25,000; V., 11,000; which according to Dureau de la Malle is equal to about $3,155, $2,333, $1,555, $800, and $388. The sixth class, the proletarians, consisted of those who possessed less and were exempt from military service and taxes. In this new assembly of centuriae (comitia centuriata) the citizens formed ranks after the manner of soldiers, in companies of one hundred (centuria), and every centuria had one vote. Now the first class placed 80 centuriae in the field; the second 22, the third 20, the fourth 22, the fifth 30 and the sixth, for propriety's sake, one. To this were added 18 centuriae of horsemen composed of the most wealthy. Hence, there were 193 centuriae, giving a lowest majority vote of 97. Now the horsemen and the first class alone had together 98 votes. Being in the majority, they had only to agree, and they could pass any resolution without asking the consent of the other classes.

This new assembly of centuriae assumed all the political rights of the former assembly of curiae, a few nominal privileges excepted. The curiae and the gentes composing them now were degraded to mere private and religious congregations, analogous to their Attic prototypes, and as such they vegetated on for a long time. But the assembly of curiae soon became obsolete. In order to drive also the three old tribes out

GENS AND STATE IN ROME

of existence, a system of four local tribes was introduced. Every tribe was assigned to one quarter of the city and received certain political rights.

Thus the old social order of blood kinship was destroyed also in Rome even before the abolition of the so-called royalty. A new constitution, founded on territorial division and difference of wealth took its place and virtually created the state. The public power of coërcion consisted here of citizens liable to military duty, to be used against the slaves and the so-called proletarians who were excluded from military service and general armament.

After the expulsion of the last rex, Tarquinius Superbus, who had really usurped royal power, the new constitution was further improved by the institution of two military leaders (consuls) with equal powers, analogous to the custom of the Iroquois. The whole history of the Roman republic moves inside of this constitution: the struggles between patricians and plebs for admission to office and participation in the allotment of state lands, the merging of the patrician nobility in the new class of large property and money owners; the gradual absorption by the latter of all the land of the small holders who had been ruined by military service; the cultivation of these enormous new tracts by slaves; the resulting depopulation of Italy which not only opened the doors to the imperial tyrants, but also to their successors, the German barbarians.

CHAPTER VII.

THE GENS AMONG CELTS AND GERMANS.

Space forbids a consideration of the gentile institutions found in a more or less pure form among the savage and barbarian races of the present day; or of the traces of such institutions, discovered in the ancient history of civilized nations in Asia. One or the other are met everywhere. A few illustrations may suffice: Even before the gens had been recognized, it was pointed out and accurately described in its main outlines by the man who took the greatest pains to misunderstand it, MacLennan, who wrote of this institution among the Kalmucks, the Circassians, the Samoyeds and three Indian nations: the Warals, the Magars and the Munnipurs. Recently it was described by M. Kovalevsky, who discovered it among the Pshavs, Shevsurs, Svanets and other Caucasian tribes. A few short notes about the existence of the gens among Celts and Germans may find a place here.

The oldest Celtic laws preserved for us still show the gens in full bloom. In Ireland, it is alive in the popular instinct to this day, after it has been forced out of actual existence by the English. It was in full force in Scotland until the middle of the eighteenth century, and here it also succumbed only to the weapons, laws and courts of the English.

The old Welsh laws, written several centuries before the English invasion, not later than the 11th century, still show collective agriculture of whole villages, although only exceptionally and as the survival of a former universal custom. Every family had five acres for its special use; another lot was at the same time

THE GENS AMONG CELTS AND GERMANS

cultivated collectively and its yield divided among the different families. In view of Irish and Scotch analogies it cannot be doubted that these village communities represent gentes or subdivisions of gentes, even though a repeated investigation of the Welsh laws, which I cannot undertake from lack of time (my notes are from 1869), should not directly corroborate this. One thing, however, is plainly proven by the Welsh and Irish laws, namely that the pairing family had not yet given way to monogamy among the Celts of the 11th century. In Wales, marriage did not become indissoluble by divorce, or rather by notification, until after seven years. Even if no more than three nights were lacking to make up the seven years, a married couple could still separate. Their property was divided among them: the woman made the division, the man selected his share. The furniture was divided according to certain very funny rules. If the marriage was dissolved by the man, he had to return the woman's dowry and a few other articles; if the woman wished a separation, then she received less. Of three children the man took two, the woman one, viz., the second child. If the woman married again after her divorce, and her first husband claimed her back, she was obliged to follow him, even if she had one foot in her new husband's bed. But if two had lived together for seven years, they were considered man and wife, even without the preliminaries of a formal marriage. Chasteness of the girls before marriage was by no means strictly observed, nor was it required. The regulations regarding this subject are of an extremely frivolous nature and in contradiction with civilized morals. When a woman committed adultery, her husband had a right to beat her—this was one of three cases when he could do so without incurring a penalty—but after that he could not demand any other satisfaction, for "the same crime

THE ORIGIN OF THE FAMILY

shall either be atoned for or avenged, but not both." The reasons that entitled a woman to a divorce without curtailing her claims to a fair settlement were of a very diverse nature: bad breath of the man was sufficient. The ransom to be paid to the chief or king for the right of the first night (gobr merch, hence the medieval name marcheta, French marquette) plays a conspicuous part in the code of laws. The women had the right to vote in the public meetings. Add to this that similar conditions are vouched for in Ireland; that marriage on time was also quite the custom there, and that the women were assured of liberal and well defined privileges in case of divorce, even to the point of remuneration for domestic services; that a "first wife" existed by the side of others, and that legal and illegal children without distinction received a share of their deceased parent's property—and we have a picture of the pairing family among the Celts. The marriage laws of the American Indians seem strict in comparison to the Celtic, but this is not surprising when we remember that the Celts were still living in group marriage at Cesar's time.

The Irish gens (Sept; the tribe was called clainne, clan) is confirmed and described not alone by the ancient law codes, but also by the English jurists of the 17th century who were sent across for the purpose of transforming the clan lands into royal dominions. Up to this time, the soil had been the collective property of the gens or the clan, except where the chiefs had already claimed it as their private dominion. When a gentile died, and a household was thus dissolved, the gentile chief (called caput cognationis by the English jurists) made a new assignment of the whole gentile territory to the rest of the household. This division of land probably took place according to such rules as were observed in Germany. Until about fifty years ago,

THE GENS AMONG CELTS AND GERMANS

village marks were quite frequent, and some of these so-called rundales may be found to this day. The farmers of a rundale, individual tenants on the soil that once was the collective property of the gens, but had been confiscated by the English conquerors, each pay the rent for his respective parcel. But they all combine their lands and parcel it off according to situation and quality. These parcels, called "Gewanne" on the German river Mosel, are cultivated collectively and their yield is divided into shares. Marshland and pastures are used in common. Fifty years ago, new divisions were still made occasionally, sometimes annually. The field map of such a rundale villege looks exactly like that of a German "Gehöferschaft" (farming commune) on the Mosel or in the Hochwald. The gens also survives in the "factions." The Irish farmers often form parties that seem to be founded on absolutely contradictory or senseless distinctions, quite incomprehensible to Englishmen. The only purpose of these factions is apparently to rally for the popular sport of hammering the life out of one another. They are artificial reincarnations, modern substitutes for the dispersed gentes that demonstrate the continuation of the old gentile instinct in their own peculiar manner. By the way, in some localities the gentiles are still living together on what is practically their old territory. During the thirties, for instance, the great majority of the inhabitants of the old county of Monaghan had only four family names, i. e., they were descended from four gentes or tribes (clans).*

Author's note to the fourth edition.
*During a few days passed in Ireland, I once more became conscious to what extent the rural population is still living in the conceptions of the gentile period. The great landholder, whose tenant the farmer is, still enjoys a position similar to that of a clan chief, who has to supervise the cultivation of the soil in the interest of all, who is entitled to a tribute from the farmer in the form of rent, but who also has to assist the farmer in cases of need. Likewise

THE ORIGIN OF THE FAMILY

The downfall of the gentile order in Scotland dates from the suppression of the revolt in 1745. What link of this order the Scotch clan represented remains to be investigated; that it is a link, is beyond doubt. Walter Scott's novels bring this Scotch highland clan vividly before our eyes. It is, as Morgan says, "an excellent type of the gens in organization and in spirit, and an extraordinary illustration of the power of the gentile life over its members. . . . We find in their feuds and blood revenge, in their localization by gentes, in their use of lands in common, in the fidelity of the clansman to his chief and of the members of the clan to each other, the usual and persistent features of gentile society. . . . Descent was in the male line, the children of the males remaining members of the clan, while the children of its female members belonged to the clans of their respective fathers." The fact that matriarchal law was formerly in force in Scotland is proved by the royal family of the Picts, who according to Beda observed female lineage. Even a survival of the Punaluan family had been preserved among the Scots, as among the Welsh. For until the middle ages, the chief of the clan or king, the last representatives of the former common husbands, had the right to claim the first night with every bride, unless a ransom was given.

It is an indisputable fact, that the Germans were

---

everyone in comfortable circumstances is considered under obligation to help his poorer neighbors whenever they are in need. Such assistance is not charity, it is simply the prerogative of the poor gentile, which the rich gentile or the chief of the clan must respect. This explains why the professors of political economy and the jurists complain of the impossibility of imparting the idea of the modern private property to the Irish farmers. Property that has only rights, but no duties, is absolutely beyond the ken of the Irishman. No wonder that so many Irishmen who are suddenly cast into one of the modern great cities of England and America, among a population with entirely different moral and legal standards, despair of all morals and justice, lose all hold and become an easy prey to demoralization.

THE GENS AMONG CELTS AND GERMANS

organized in gentes up to the time of the great migrations. The territory between the Danube, the Rhine, the Vistula and the northern seas was evidently occupied by them only a few centuries before Christ. The Cimbri and Teutons were then still in full migration, and the Suebi did not settle down until Cesar's time. Cesar expressly states that they settled down in gentes and kins (gentibus cognatibusque), and in the mouth of a Roman of the gens Julia this term gentibus has a definite meaning, that no amount of disputation can obliterate. This holds good for all Germans. It seems that even the provinces taken by them from the Romans were settled by distribution to gentes. The Alemanian code of laws affirms that the people settled in gentes (genealogiae) on the conquered land south of the Danube. Genealogia is used in exactly the same sense as was later on Mark—or Dorfgenossenschaft (mark or village community). Kovalevsky recently maintained that these genealogiae were the great household communities among which the land was divided, and from which the village communities developed later on. The same may be true of the fara, by which term the Burgundians and Langobards—a Gothic and a Herminonian or High German tribe—designated nearly, if not exactly, the same thing as the Alemanian genealogiae. Whether this is really the gens or the household community, must be settled by further investigation.

The language records leave us in doubt, whether all the Germans had a common expression for gens or not, and as to what this term was. Etymologically, the Gothic, kuni, middle High German künne, corresponds to the Grecian genos and the Latin gens, and is used in the same sense. We are led back to the time of matriarchy by the terms for "woman" which are derived from the same root: Greek gynê, Slav zenâ, Gothic qvino, Norse kona, kuna.

THE ORIGIN OF THE FAMILY

Among Langobards and Burgundians, I repeat, we find the term fara which Grimm derives from the hypothetical root fisan, to beget. I should prefer to trace it to the more obvious root faran, German fahren, to ride or to wander, in order to designate a certain well defined section of the wandering corps, composed quite naturally of relatives. As a result of centuries of wanderings from West to East and back again, this term was gradually applied to the sex group itself.

There is furthermore the Gothic sibja, Anglosaxon sib, old High German sippia, sippa, High German sippe. Old Norse has only the plural sifjar, the relatives; the singular occurs only as the name of a goddess, Sif.

Finally, another expression occurs in the Hildebrand Song, where Hildebrand asks Hadubrand "who is your father among the men of the nation . . . or what is your kin?" (eddo huêllihhes cnuosles du sis).

If there was a common German term for gens, it was presumably the Gothic kuni. This is not only indicated by its identity with the corresponding term in related languages, but also by the fact that the word kuning, German König, English king, is derived from it, all of which originally signified chief of gens or tribe. Sibja, German Sippe (relationship), does not appear worthy of consideration. In old Norse, at least, sifjar signifies not alone kin by blood, but also kin through marriage; hence it comprises the members of at least two gentes, and the term sif cannot have been applied to the gens itself.

In the order of battle, the Germans, like the Mexicans and Greeks, arranged the horsemen as well as the wedge-like columns of the troops on foot by gentes. Tacitus' indefinite expression, "by families and kinships," is explained by the fact that at his time the gens had long ceased to be a living body in Rome.

THE GENS AMONG CELTS AND GERMANS

Another passage of Tacitus is decisive. There he says: "The mother's brother regards his nephew as his son; some even hold that the bond of blood between the maternal uncle and the nephew is more sacred and close than that between father and son, so that when persons are demanded as securities, the sister's son is considered a better security than the natural son of the man whom they desire to place under bonds." Here we have a living proof of the matriarchal, and hence natural, gens, and it is described as a characteristic mark of the Germans.* If a member of such a gens gave his own son as a security for the fulfillment of a vow and this son became the victim of his father's breach of faith, that was the concern of the father alone. But when the son of a sister was sacrificed, then the most sacred gentile law was violated. The next relative who was bound above all others to protect the boy or young man, was held responsible for his death; either he should not have given the boy in bail or he should have kept the contract. If we had no other trace of gentile law among the Germans, this one pasage would be sufficient proof of its existence.

But there is another passage in the Old Norse song of the "Dawn of the Gods" and the "End of the

---

Author's note.
*The Greeks know this special sacredness of the bond between the mother's brother and his nephew, a relic of maternal law found among many nations, only in the mythology of heroic times. According to Diodorus IV., 34, Meleagros kills the sons of Thestius, the brother of his mother Althaia. The latter regards this deed as such a heinous crime that she curses the murderer, her own son, and prays for his death. "It is said that the gods fulfilled her wish and ended the life of Meleagros." According to the same Diordorus, IV., 44, the Argonauts under Herakles land in Thracia and there find that Phineus, at the instigation of his second wife, shamefully maltreats his two sons, the offspring of his first deserted wife, the Boread Kleopatra. But among the Argonauts there are also some Boreads, the brothers of Kleopatra, the uncles of the maltreated boys. They at once champion their nephews, set them free and kill their guards.

THE ORIGIN OF THE FAMILY

World," the Völuspâ, which is still stronger evidence, because it is 800 years younger. In this "Vision of the Seeress," in which Bang and Bugge have now demonstrated the existence of Christian elements, also, the description of the time of general degeneration and corruption inaugurating the great catastrophe contains this passage:

Broedbr munu berjask ok at bönum verdask
Munu systrungar sifjum spilla.

"Brothers will wage war against one another and become each other's murderers, and sisters' children will break the bonds of blood." Systrungr means the son of the mother's sister, and an abnegation of the blood kinship from that side surpasses in the eyes of the poet even the crime of fratricide. There is a deliberate climax in that systrungar, emphasizing the maternal kinship. If the term syskina-börn, brother's and sister's children, or syskina-synir, brother's and sister's sons, had been used, there would have been a weakening of the effect, instead of a climax. That shows that even at the time of the Vikings, when the Völuspâ was composed, the recollection of maternal law was not yet blotted out.

Among the Germans with whom Tacitus was familiar maternal law had already given way to paternal lineage. The children were the next heirs of the father; in the absence of children, the brothers and uncles on both sides were next in line. The admission of the mother's brother to the inheritance is a relic of maternal law and proves that paternal law had only recently been introduced by the Germans. Traces of maternal law were preserved until late in the middle ages. It seems that even at this late date people still felt certain misgivings about the reliability of fatherhood, especially among serfs. For when a feudal lord demanded the return of a fugitive serf from a city, it was first required, for

THE GENS AMONG CELTS AND GERMANS

instance in Augsburg, Basel and Kaiserslautern, that the fact of his serfdom should be established by the oaths of six of his next blood relations, all of whom had to belong to his mother's kin. (Maurer, Städteverfassung, I, page 381.)

Another relic of declining matriarchy was the (from the Roman standpoint) almost inexplicable respect of the Germans for the female sex. Young girls of noble family were considered the safest bonds to secure the keeping of contracts with Germans. In battle, nothing stimulated their courage so much as the horrible thought that their wives and daughters might be captured and carried into slavery. A woman was to them something holy and prophetical, and they listened to her advice in the most important matters. Veleda, the Bructerian priestess on the river Lippe, was the soul of the insurrection of the Batavians, in which Civilis at the head of German and Belgian tribes shook the foundations of Roman rule in Gaul. The women held undisputed sway in the house. If we may believe Tacitus, they, together with the old men and children, had to do all the work, for the men went hunting, drank and loafed. But as Tacitus does not say who cultivated the fields, and as according to his explicit statement the slaves paid only tithes, but did not work under compulsion, it seems that the adult men would have had to do what little agricultural work was required.

The form of marriage, as stated above, was the pairing family in gradual transition to monogamy. It was not yet strict monogamy, for polygamy was permitted for the wealthy. Chasteness of the girls was in general carefully maintained, different from the custom of the Celts. Tacitus speaks with special ardor of the sacredness of the matrimonial bond among the Germans. Adultery of the woman is alone quoted by him as a reason for a divorce. But

THE ORIGIN OF THE FAMILY

his treatment of this subject leaves many a flaw and besides, it too openly holds up the mirror of virtue to the dissipated Romans. So much is certain: Granted that the Germans were such exceptional models of virtue in their forests, it required only a short contact with the outer world to bring them down to the level of the other average Europeans. In the whirl of Roman life the last trace of pure morals disappeared even faster than the German language. Just read Gregorius of Tours. It is obvious that in the primeval forests of Germany no such hyper-refined voluptuousness could exist as in Rome. That implies fully enough superiority of the Germans over the Roman world, and there is no necessity for ascribing to them a moderation and chastity that have never been the qualities of any nation as a whole.

A result of gentile law is the obligation to inherit the enmities as well as the friendships of one's father and relatives; so is furthermore the displacement of blood revenge by the Wergeld, a fine to be paid in atonement of manslaughter and injuries. A generation ago this Wergeld was considered a specifically German institution, but it has since been found that hundreds of nations introduced this mitigation of gentile blood revenge. Like the obligatory hospitality, it is found, for instance, among the American Indians. Tacitus' description of the manner in which hospitality was observed (Germania, chapt. 21) is almost identical with Morgan's.

The hot and ceaseless controversy as to whether or not the Germans had already made a definite repartition of the cultivated land at Tacitus' time, and how the passages relating to this question should be interpreted, is now a thing of the past. After the following facts had been established: that the cultivated land of nearly all nations was tilled collec-

THE GENS AMONG CELTS AND GERMANS

tively by the gens and later on by communistic family groups, a practice which Cesar still found among the Suebi; that as a result of this practice the land was re-apportioned periodically; and that this periodical repartition of the cultivated land was preserved in Germany down to our days—after such evidence we need not waste any more breath on the subject. A transition within 150 years from collective cultivation, such as Cesar expressly attributes to the Suebi, to individual cultivation with annual repartition of the soil, such as Tacitus found among the Germans, is surely progress enough for any one. The further transition from this stage to complete private ownership of land during such a short period and without any external intervention would involve an absolute impossibility. Hence I can only read in Tacitus what he states in so many words: They change (or re-divide) the cultivated land every year, and enough land is left for common use. It is the stage of agriculture and appropriation of the soil which exactly tallies with the contemporaneous gentile constitution of the Germans.

I leave the preceding paragraph unchanged, just as it stood in former editions. Meantime the question has assumed another aspect. Since Kovalevsky has demonstrated that the patriarchal household community existed nearly everywhere, perhaps even everywhere, as the connecting link between the matriarchal communistic and the modern isolated family, the question is no longer "Collective property or private property?" as discussed between Maurer and Waitz, but "What was the form of that collective property?" Not alone is there no doubt whatever, that the Suebi were the collective owners of their land at Cesar's time, but also that they tilled the soil collectively. The questions, whether their economic unit was the gens, or the household, or an intermedi-

THE ORIGIN OF THE FAMILY

ate communistic group, or whether all three of these groups existed at the same time as a result of different local conditions, may remain undecided for a long while yet. Kovalevsky maintains that the conditions described by Tacitus were not founded on the mark or village community, but on the household community, which developed much later into the village community by the growth of the population.

Hence the settlements of the Germans on the territory they occupied at the time of the Romans, and on territory later taken by them from the Romans, would not have consisted of villages, but of large co-operative families comprising several generations, who cultivated a sufficient piece of land and used the surrounding wild land in common with their neighbors. If this was the case, then the passage in Tacitus regarding the changing of the cultivated land would indeed have an agronomic meaning, viz., that the co-operative household cultivated a different piece of land every year, and the land cultivated during the previous year was left untilled or entirely abandoned. The scarcity of the population would have left enough spare wild lands to make all dispute about land unnecessary. Only after the lapse of centuries, when the members of the family had increased so that the collective cultivation became incompatible with the prevailing conditions of production, the household communities were dissolved. The former common fields and meadows were then divided in the well-known manner among the various individual families that had now formed. The division of farm lands was first periodical, but later final, while forest, pasture and watercourses remained common property.

It seems that this process of development has been fully established for Russia by historical investigation. As for Germany and, in the second place, for

THE GENS AMONG CELTS AND GERMANS

other German countries, it cannot be denied that this view affords in many instances a better interpretation of historical authorities and a readier solution of difficulties than the idea of tracing the village community to the time of Tacitus. The oldest documents, e. g. of the Codex Laureshamensis, are easier explained by the help of the household than of the village community. On the other hand, new difficulties now arise and new questions pose themselves. It will require further investigations to arrive at definite conclusions. However, I cannot deny that the probability is very much in favor of the intermediate stage of the household community.*

While the Germans of Cesar's time had either just taken up settled abodes, or were still looking for them, they had been settled for a full century at the time of Tacitus. As a result there is a manifest progress in the production of necessities. The Germans lived in block houses; their clothing was still as primitive as their forests, consisting of rough woolen cloaks, animal skins and linen underclothing

---

Translator's note.
*The household community is still a distinct stage of production in Georgia (South Russia). The northern boundary of Georgia is the Caucasus. The Georgians, a people of high intelligence, have for centuries maintained their independence against Persians, Arabs, Turcs and Tartars. Dr. Philipp Gogitshayshvili gives the following interesting description of their condition in an article, entitled "Das Gewerbe in Georgien" (Zeitschrift fur die gesammte Staatswissenschaft, Erganzungsheft I., Tubingen, 1901). "The Swanians (a district of Georgia is called Swania) have all the necessities of life. They weave their own clothing, make their own weapons, powder and even silver, and gold ornaments. There is no modern trading . . . . . They are acquainted with exchange, but only of products for products. Money does not circulate and there are neither shops nor markets. . . . . There is not a single beggar, not a single man who asks for charity. With the exception of iron, salt and chintz, the Swanians produce all they need themselves. They prepare their linen from hemp, their clothing from skins of wild animals and wool, their footwear from hides and leather. They make feltcaps, household goods, weapons, saddles, bridles and agricultural implements."

THE ORIGIN OF THE FAMILY

for the women and the wealthy. They lived on milk, meat, wild fruit and, as Pliny adds, oatmeal porridge which is the Celtic national dish in Ireland and Scotland to-day. Their wealth consisted in cattle of an inferior race. The kine were small, of unattractive appearance and without horns; the horses, little ponies, were not fast runners. Money, Roman coin only, was rarely used. They did not make ornaments of gold and silver, nor did they value these metals. Iron was scarce and, at least among the tribes on the Rhine and the Danube, was apparently only imported, not mined by themselves. The Runen script (imitations of Greek and Latin letters) was only used as a cipher and exclusively for religious sorcery. Human sacrifices were still in vogue. In short, they were a nation just emerged out of the middle stage of barbarism into the upper stage. But while the tribes whose immediate contact with the Romans facilitated the import of Roman products, were thereby prevented from acquiring a metal and textile industry of their own, there is not the least doubt that the tribes of the Northeast, on the Baltic, developed these industries. The pieces of armor found in the bogs of Sleswick—a long iron sword, a coat of mail, a silver helmet, etc., together with Roman coins from the close of the second century—, and the German metal ware spread by the migrations represent a peculiar type of a superior finish, even such as were modeled after Roman originals. With the exception of England, the emigration into the civilized Roman empire everywhere put an end to this home industry. How simultaneously this industry arose and developed, is shown e. g. by the bronze spangles. The specimens found in Burgundy, in Roumania and on the Sea of Asow, might have been manufactured in the same shop with those

THE GENS AMONG CELTS AND GERMANS

found in England or Sweden and are of undoubted German origin.

The German constitution was also in keeping with the upper stage of barbarism. According to Tacitus, the council of chiefs (principes) universally decided matters of minor importance and prepared important matters for the decision of the public meetings. So far as we know anything of the public meeting in the lower stage of barbarism, viz., among the American Indians, it was only held by gentes, not by tribes or leagues of tribes. The chiefs of peace (principes) were still sharply distinguished from the chiefs of war (duces), just as among the Iroquois. The peace chiefs were already living in part on honorary donations of the gentiles, such as cattle, grain, etc. They were generally elected from the same family, analogous to America. The transition to paternal law favored, as in Greece and Rome, the gradual transformation of office by election into hereditary office. A "noble" family was thus gradually raised in each gens. Most of this hereditary nobility came to grief during the migrations or shortly after. The military leaders were elected solely on their merits. They had little power and were obliged to rely on the force of their example. The actual disciplinary power in the army was held by the priests, as Tacitus implicitly states. The public meeting was the real executive. The king or chief of the tribe presided. The people decided. A murmur signified "No," acclamation and clanging of weapons meant "Yes." The public meeting was at the same time a court of justice. Complaints were here brought forth and decided, and death sentences pronounced. Only cowardice, treason and unnatural lust were capital crimes. The gentes and other subdivisions decided in a body under the chairmanship of the chief, who in all original German courts was only the manager

THE ORIGIN OF THE FAMILY

of the transactions and questioner. Among Germans, the sentence has ever and everywhere been pronounced by the community.

Leagues of tribes came into existence since Cesar's time. Some of them already had kings. The first chief of war began to covet the usurper's place, as among Greeks and Romans, and sometimes succeeded in obtaining it. Such successful usurpers were by no means absolute rulers. But still they began to break through the bonds of the gens. While freed slaves generally occupied an inferior position, because they could not be members of any gens, they often gained rank, wealth and honors as favorites of the new kings. The same thing took place after the conquest of the Roman empire by those military leaders who had now become kings of great countries. Among the Frankons, slaves and freed slaves of the king played a leading role first at the court, then in the state. A large part of the new nobility were descended from them.

There was one institution that especially favored the rise of royalty: the military following. We have already seen, how among the American redskins private war groups were formed independently of the gens. Among the Germans, these private groups had developed into standing bodies. The military leader who had acquired fame, gathered around his person a host of booty loving young warriors. They were pledged to personal faithfulness by their leader who in return pledged himself to them. He fed them, gave them presents and organized them on hierarchic principles: a body guard and a troop for immediate emergencies and short expeditions, a trained corps of officers for larger enterprises. These followings must have been rather insignificant, in fact we find them so later under Odoaker in Italy, still they portended the decay of the old gentile liberty, and the

THE GENS AMONG CELTS AND GERMANS

events during and after the migrations proved that military retainers were heralds of evil. For in the first place, they fostered the growth of royalty. In the second place, Tacitus affirms that they could only be held together by continual warfare and plundering expeditions. Robbery became their life purpose. If the leader found nothing to do in his neighborhood, he marched his troops to other countries, where a prospect of war and booty allured him. The German auxiliaries, many of whom fought under the Roman standard even against Germans, had been largely recruited among such followings. They represent the first germs of the "Landsknecht" profession, the shame and curse of the Germans. After the conquest of the Roman empire, these retainers of kings together with the unfree Roman courtiers formed the other half of the nobility of later days.

In general, then, the German tribes combined into nations had the same constitution that had developed among the Greeks of the heroic era and the Romans at the time of the so-called kings: public meetings, councils of gentile chiefs and military leaders who coveted actual royal power. It was the highest constitution which the gentile order could produce; it was the standard constitution of the higher stage of barbarism. If society passed the limits for which this constitution sufficed, then the end of the gentile order had come. It collapsed and the state took its place.

CHAPTER VIII.

THE RISE OF THE STATE AMONG GERMANS.

According to Tacitus the German nation was very strong in numbers. An approximate idea of the strength of individual German nations is given by Caesar. He states that the number of Usipetans and Tencterans who crossed over to the left bank of the Rhine amounted to 180,000, including women and children. About 100,000* members to a single nation is considerably more than e. g. the Iroquois numbered in their prime, when 20,000 of them became the terror of the whole country, from the Great Lakes to the Ohio and Potomac. If we attempt to place the better known nations of the Rhine country by the help of historical reports, we find that a single nation occupies on the map the average area of a Prussian government district, about 10,000 square kilometers* or 182 German geographical square miles.** The Germania Magna of the Romans, reaching to the Vistula, comprised about 500,000 square kilometers. Counting an average of 100,000

Author's note.

*The number assumed here is confirmed by a passage of Diodorus on the Celts of Gaul: "Many nations of unequal strength are living in Gaul. The strongest of them numbers about 200,000, the weakest 50,000." (Diodorus Siculus, V., 25.) That gives an average of 125,000. The individual nations of Gaul, being more highly developed, should be gauged more numerous than those of Germany.

Translator's note.

*3861 square statute miles.

**A German geographical mile contains 7,420.44 meters, or 7,42044 kilometers: hence a German geographical square mile contains 55.0629 square kilometers, equal to 21.2592 square statute miles.

RISE OF THE STATE AMONG GERMANS

for any single nation, the total population of Germania Magna would have amounted to five millions. This is a rather high figure for a barbarian group of nations, although 10 inhabitants to the square kilometer or 550 to the geographical square mile is very little when compared to present conditions. But this does not include the whole number of Germans then living. We know that German nations of the Gothic race, Bastarnians, Peukinians and others, lived all along the Carpathian mountains away down to the mouth of the Danube. They were so numerous that Pliny designated them as the fifth main division of the Germans. As much as 180 years B. C. they were mercenaries of the Macedonian King Perseus, and during the first years of Augustus they were still pushing their way as far as the vicinity of Adrianople. Assuming them to have been one million strong we find that at least six millions was the probable population of Germany at the beginning of the Christian era.

After the final settlement in Germany, the population must have grown with increasing rapidity. The industrial progress mentioned above would be sufficient to prove it. The objects found in the bogs of Sleswick, to judge by the Roman coins found with them, are from the third century. Hence at that time the metal and textile industry was already well developed on the Baltic, a lively traffic with the Roman empire was carried on, and the wealthier class enjoyed a certain luxury—all of which indicates that the population had increased. But at the same time the general war of aggression against the Romans commenced along the whole line of the Rhine, of the Roman wall and of the Danube, a line stretching from the North Sea to the Black Sea. This is another proof of the ever growing outward pressure of the population. During the struggle which lasted three

THE ORIGIN OF THE FAMILY

centuries, the whole main body of the Gothic nations, with the exception of the Scandinavian Goths and the Burgundians, marched to the Southeast and formed the left wing of the long line of attack. The High Germans (Herminonians) on the Upper Danube fought in the center, and the Iskaevonians on the Rhine, now called Franks, advanced on the right wing. The conquest of Brittany fell to the lot of the Ingaevonians.* At the end of the fifth century, the exhausted, bloodless, and helpless Roman empire lay open to the Germans.

In former chapters we stood at the cradle of antique Greek and Roman civilization. Now we are standing at its grave. The equalizing plane of Roman world power had been gliding for centuries over all the Mediterranean countries. Where the Greek language did not offer any resistance, all national idioms had been crushed by a corrupted Latin. There were no longer any distinctions of nationality, no more Gauls, Iberians, Ligurians, Noricans; they had all become Romans. Roman administration and Roman law had everywhere dissolved the old gentile bodies and thus crushed the last remnant of local and national independence. The new type of Romans offered no compensation for this loss, for it did not express any nationality, but only the lack of a nationality. The elements for the formation of new nations were present everywhere. The Latin dialects of the different provinces differentiated more and more. But the natural boundaries that had once made Italy, Gaul, Spain, Africa independent territories, were still present and made themselves felt. Yet there was no strength anywhere for combining

---

Translator's note.

*The Ingaevonians comprised the Friesians, the Saxons, the Jutes and the Angles, living on the coast of the North Sea from the Zuider Zee to Denmark.

RISE OF THE STATE AMONG GERMANS

these elements into new nations. Nowhere was there the least trace of any capacity for development, nor any power of resistance, much less any creative power. The immense human throng of that enormous territory was held together by one bond alone: the Roman state. But this state had in time become the worst enemy and oppressor of its subjects. The provinces had ruined Rome. It had become a provincial town like all others, **privileged**, but no longer ruling, no longer the center of the world empire, no longer even the seat of the emperors and subregents who lived in Constantinople, Treves and Milan. The Roman state had become an immense complicated machine, designed exclusively for the exploitation of its subjects. Taxes, state imposts and tithes of all sorts drove the mass of the people deeper and deeper into poverty. By the blackmailing practices of the regents, tax collectors and soldiers, the pressure was increased to such a point that it became insupportable. This was the outcome of Rome's world power. The right of the state to existence was founded on the preservation of order in the interior and the protection against the barbarians outside. But this order was worse than the most disgusting disorder, and the barbarians against whom the state pretended to protect its citizens, were hailed by them as saviors.

The condition of society was no less desperate. During the last years of the republic, the Roman rulers had already contrived the pitiless exploitation of the conquered provinces. The emperors had not abolished, but organized this exploitation. The more the empire fell to pieces, the higher rose the taxes and tithes, and the more shamelessly did the officials rob and blackmail. Commerce and industry had never been a strong point of the domineering Romans. Only in usury they had excelled all other nations before and after them. What commerce had managed to exist, had been ruined by official extortion. Only in the East, in the Grecian part of the empire, some commerce still vegetated, but this is outside of the scope of our study. Universal reduction to poverty, decrease of traffic, of handicrafts, of art, of population, decay of the towns, return of agriculture to a lower stage—that had been the final result of Roman world supremacy.

But now agriculture, the most prominent branch of production in the whole Old World, was again supreme, and more than ever. In Italy, the immense estates (latifundiae) that comprised nearly the whole country since the end of the republic, had been utilized in two ways: either as pastures on which the population had been replaced by sheep and oxen, the care of which required only a few slaves; or as country seats, on which masses of slaves carried on horticulture on a large scale, partly for the luxury of the owner, partly for sale on the markets of the towns. The great pastures had been preserved and even extended in certain parts. But the country seats and their horticulture had gone to ruin through the impoverishment of their owners and the decay of the towns. Latifundian economy based on slave labor was no longer profitable; but in its time it had been the only possible form of agriculture on a large scale. Now, however, small production had again become the only lucrative form. One country seat after the other was parceled and leased in small lots to hereditary tenants who paid a fixed rent, or to partiarii, more administrators than tenants who received one-sixth or even only one-ninth of a year's product in remuneration for their work. But these little lots were principally disposed of to colonists who paid a fixed sum annually and could be transferred by sale together with their lots. Although no

RISE OF THE STATE AMONG GERMANS

slaves, still these colonists were not free; they could not marry free citizens, and marriages with members of their own class were not regarded as valid, but as mere concubinages like those of the slaves. The colonists were the prototypes of the medieval serfs.

The ancient slavery had lost its vitality. Neither in the country in large scale agriculture, nor in the manufactories of the towns did it yield any more returns—the market for its products had disappeared. And small scale production and artisanship, to which the gigantic production of the flourishing time of the empire was now reduced, did not leave any room for numerous slaves. Only house and luxury slaves of the rich were still retained by society. But this declining slavery was as yet sufficiently strong to brand productive labor as slave work, as below the dignity of free Romans; and everybody was now a free Roman. An increasing number of superfluous slaves who had become a drug on their owners were dismissed, while on the other hand the number of colonists and of beggared free men (similar to the poor whites in the slave states of America) grew continuously. Christianity is perfectly innocent of this gradual decline of ancient slavery. For it had taken part in the slavery of the Roman empire for centuries. It never prevented the slave trade of Christians later on, neither of the Germans in the North, nor of the Venetians on the Mediterranean, nor the negro traffic of later years.* Slavery died, because it did not pay any longer. But it left behind its poisonous sting by branding as ignoble the productive labor of free men.

Author's note.
*According to Bishop Liutprand of Cremona, the main industry of Verdun in the tenth century, in the so-called Holy German Empire, was the manufacture of eunuchs, who were exported with great profit to Spain for the harems of the Moors.

THE ORIGIN OF THE FAMILY

This brought the Roman world into a closed alley from which it could not escape. Slave labor was economically impossible and the labor of free men was under a moral ban. The one could exist no longer, the other could not yet be the fundamental form of social production. There was no other help but a complete revolution.

The provinces were not any better off. The most complete reports on this subject are from Gaul. By the side of the colonists, free farmers still existed there. In order to protect themselves against the brutal blackmail of the officials, judges and usurers, they frequently placed themselves under the protectorate of a man of influence and power. Not only single individuals did so, but whole communities, so that the emperors of the fourth century often issued decrees prohibiting this practice. But what good did protection do to the clients? The patron imposed the condition that they should transfer the title of their lots to him, and in return he assured them of the free enjoyment of their land for life—a trick which the holy church remembered and freely imitated during the ninth and tenth century, for the greater glory of God. In the fifth century, however, about the year 475, Bishop Salvianus of Marseilles still vehemently denounced such robbery and relates that the methods of the Roman officials and great landlords became so oppressive that many "Romans" fled to the districts occupied by the barbarians and feared nothing so much as a return under Roman rule. That poor parents frequently sold their children into slavery, is proved by a law forbidding this practice.

In return for liberating the Romans from their own state, the barbarians appropriated two-thirds of the entire land and divided it among themselves. The distribution was made by gentile rules. As the number of the conquerors was relatively small, large

RISE OF THE STATE AMONG GERMANS

tracts remained undivided in the possession of the nation, the tribe or the gens. Every gens distributed the land for cultivation and pastures to the individual households by drawing lots. We do not know whether repeated divisions took place at that time. At any rate, this practice was soon discarded in the Roman provinces, and the individual lot became salable private property, a so-called freehold (allodium). Forests and pastures remained undivided for collective use. This use and the mode of cultivating the divided land was regulated by tradition and the will of the community. The longer the gens lived in its village, and the better Germans and Romans became amalgamated in the course of time, the more did the character of kinship lose ground before territorial bounds. The gens disappeared in the mark commune, the members of which, however, still exhibited traces of kinship. In the countries where mark communes were still preserved—in the North of France, in England, Germany and Scandinavia—the gentile constitution gradually merged into a local constitution and thus acquired the capacity of being fitted into a state. Nevertheless this local constitution retained some of the primeval democratic character which distinguishes the whole gentile order, and thus preserved a piece of gentilism even in its enforced degeneration of later times. This left a weapon in the hands of the oppressed, ready to be wielded by them even in the present time.

The rapid loss of the bonds of blood in the gens as a result of conquest caused the degeneration of the tribal and national organs of gentilism. We know that the rule over subjugated people does not agree with the gentile constitution. Here we have an opportunity to observe this on a large scale. The German nations, masters of the Roman provinces, had to organize their conquests. But they could

THE ORIGIN OF THE FAMILY

neither adopt the Romans as a body into their gentes, nor rule them by the help of gentile organs. A substitute for them had to be placed at the head of the Roman administrative bodies that were largely retained in local affairs, and this substitute could only be another state. Hence the organs of the gentile constitution had to become organs of the state, and under the pressure of the moment this took place very rapidly. Now the first representative of the conquering nation was the military leader. The internal and external security of the conquered territory demanded that his power should be strengthened. The moment had arrived for the transition from war leadership to monarchy. And the change took place.

Take e. g. the realm of the Franks. The victorious Salians had not only come into possession of the extensive Roman state dominions, but also of all the large tracts that had not been assigned to the more or less small mark communities, especially of all large forest tracts. The first thing which the king of the Franks, now a real monarch, did was to change this national property into royal property, to steal it from the people and to donate or give it in lien to his retainers. This retinue, originally composed of his personal war followers and of the sub-commanders of the army, was increased by Romans, i. e., romanized Gauls who quickly became invaluable to the king through their knowledge of writing, their education and their familiarity with the language and laws of the country, and with the language of Latin literature. But slaves, serfs and freed slaves also became his courtiers. From among all these he chose his favorites. At first they received donations of public land, and later on these benefits were generally conferred for the lifetime of the king. The foundation of a new nobility was thus laid at the expense of the people.

RISE OF THE STATE AMONG GERMANS

But this was not all. The wide expanse of the empire could not be governed by means of the old gentile constitution. The council of chiefs, if it had not become obsolete long ago, could not have held any more meetings. It was soon displaced by the standing retinue of the king. A pretense at the old public meeting was still kept up, but it also was more and more limited to the meeting of the subcommanders of the army and the rising nobles.

Just as formerly, the Roman farmers during the last period of the republic, so now the free land-owning peasants, the mass of the Frank people, were exhausted and reduced to penury by continual civil feuds and wars of conquest. They who once had formed the whole army and, after the conquest of France, its picked body, were so impoverished at the end of the ninth century that hardly more than every fifth man could go to war. The former army of free peasants, convoked directly by the king, was replaced by an army composed of dependents of the new nobles. Among these servants were also villeins, the descendants of the peasants who had acknowledged no master but the king and a little earlier not even a king. Under Charlemagne's successors the ruin of the Frank peasantry was aggravated by internal wars, weakness of the royal power and corresponding overbearance of the nobles. The latter had received another addition to their ranks through the installation by Charlemagne of "Gau" * (district) counts who strove to make their offices hereditary. The invasions of the Normans completed the wreck of the peasantry. Fifty years after the death of Charlemagne, France lay as resistless at the feet of the Normans, as four hundred years pre-

---
Translator's note.
*The "Gau" is a larger territory than the "Mark." Caesar and Tacitus called it pagus.

THE ORIGIN OF THE FAMILY

vious the Roman empire had lain at the feet of the Franks.

Not only was the external impotence almost the same, but also the internal order or rather disorder of society. The free Frank peasants found themselves in a similar position as their predecessors, the Roman colonists. Ruined by wars and robberies, they had been forced to seek the protection of the nobles or the church, because the royal power was too weak to shield them. But they had to pay dearly for this protection. Like the Gallic farmers, they had to transfer the titles of their land to their patrons, and received it back from them as tenants in different and varying forms, but always only in consideration of services and tithes. Once driven into this form of dependence, they gradually lost their individual liberty. After a few generations most of them became serfs. How rapidly the free peasants sank from their level is shown by the land records of the abbey Saint Germain des Prés, then near, now in, Paris. On the vast holdings of this abbey in the surrounding country 2788 households, nearly all of them Franks with German names, were living at Charlemagne's time; 2080 of them were colonists, 35 lites,* 220 slaves and only 8 freeholders. The practice of the patrons to demand the transfer of the land titles to themselves and give the former owners the use of the land for life, denounced as ungodly by Salvianus, was now universally practiced by the Church in its dealings with the peasants. The compulsory labor that now came more and more into vogue, had been moulded as much after the Roman angariae, compulsory service for the state, as after the services of the German mark men in bridge and road building and other work for common pur-

---
Translator's note.
*The name given in ancient law to dependent farmers.

RISE OF THE STATE AMONG GERMANS

poses. By all appearances, then, the mass of the population had arrived at the same old goal after four hundred years.

That proved two things: Firstly, that the social differentiation and the division of property in the sinking Roman empire corresponded perfectly to the contemporaneous stage of production in agriculture and industry, and hence was unavoidable; secondly, that this stage of production had not been essentially altered for better or worse during four hundred years, and therefore had necessarily produced the same division of property and the same classes of population. The town had lost its supremacy over the country during the last centuries of the Roman empire, and had not regained it during the first centuries of German rule. This presupposes a low stage of agriculture and industry. Such a general condition produces of necessity the domination of great proprietors and the dependence of small farmers. How impossible it was to graft either the slave labor of Roman latifundian economy or the compulsory labor of the new large scale production into such a society, is proved by Charlemagne's very extensive experiments with his famous imperial country residences that left hardly a trace. These experiments were continued only by the convents and brought results only for them. But the convents were abnormal social institutions, founded on celibacy. They could do exceptional work, but they had to remain exceptions themselves for this very reason.

Yet some progress had been made during these four hundred years. Although in the end we find the same main classes as in the beginning, still the human beings that made up these classes had changed. The ancient slavery had disappeared; gone were also the beggared freemen who had despised work as slavish. Between the Roman colonist and

THE ORIGIN OF THE FAMILY

the new serf, there had been the free Frank peasant. The "useless remembrance and the vain feud" of the decaying Roman nation was dead and gone. The social classes of the ninth century had been formed during the travail of a new civilization, not in the demoralization of a sinking one. The new race, masters and servants, were a race of men as compared to their Roman predecessors. The relation of powerful landlords to serving peasants, which had been the unavoidable result of collapse in the antique world, was for the Franks the point of departure on a new line of development. Moreover, unproductive as these four hundred years may appear, they left behind one great product: the modern nationalities, the reorganization and differentiation of West European humanity for the coming history. The Germans had indeed infused a new life into Europe. Therefore the dissolution of the states in the German period did not end in a subjugation after the Norse-Saracene plan, but in a continued development of the estate of the royal beneficiaries and an increasing submission (commendatio) to feudalism, and in such a tremendous increase of the population, that no more than two centuries later the bloody drain of the crusades could be sustained without injury.

What was the mysterious charm by which the Germans infused a new life into decrepit Europe? Was it an innate magic power of the German race, as our jingo historians would have it? By no means. Of course, the Germans were a highly gifted Aryan branch and, especially at that time, in full process of vigorous development. They did not, however, rejuvenate Europe by their specific national properties, but simply by their barbarism, their gentile constitution.

Their personal efficiency and bravery, their love of liberty, and their democratic instinct which re-

RISE OF THE STATE AMONG GERMANS

garded all public affairs as its own affairs, in short all those properties which the Romans had lost and which were alone capable of forming new states and raising new nationalities out of the muck of the Roman world—what were they but characteristic marks of the barbarians in the upper stage, fruits of the gentile constitution?

If they transformed the antique form of monogamy, mitigated the male rule in the family and gave a higher position to women than the classic world had ever known, what enabled them to do so, unless it was their barbarism, their gentile customs, their living inheritance of the time of maternal law?

If they could safely transmit a trace of the genuine gentile order, the mark communes, to the feudal states of at least three of the most important countries—Germany, North of France, and England—and thus give a local coherence and the means of resistance to the oppressed class, the peasants, even under the hardest medieval serfdom; means which neither the slaves of antiquity nor the modern proletarian found ready at hand—to whom did they owe this, unless it was again their barbarism, their exclusively barbarian mode of settling in gentes?

And in conclusion, if they could develop and universally introduce the mild form of servitude which they had been practicing at home, and which more and more displaced slavery also in the Roman empire—to whom was it due, unless it was again their barbarism thanks to which they had not yet arrived at complete slavery, neither in the form of the ancient labor slaves, nor in that of the oriental house slaves?

This milder form of servitude, as Fourier first stated, gave to the oppressed the means of their gradual emancipation as a class (fournit aux cultivateurs des moyens d'affranchissement collectif et

THE ORIGIN OF THE FAMILY

progressif) and is therefore far superior to slavery, which permits only the immediate enfranchisement of the individual without any transitory stage. Antiquity did not know any abolition of slavery by rebellion, but the serfs of the middle ages gradually enforced their liberation as a class.

Every vital and productive germ with which the Germans inoculated the Roman world, was due to barbarism. Indeed, only barbarians are capable of rejuvenating a world laboring under the death throes of unnerved civilization. And the higher stage of barbarism, to which and in which the Germans worked their way up previous to the migrations, was best calculated to prepare them for this work. That explains everything.

CHAPTER IX.

BARBARISM AND CIVILIZATION.

Having observed the dissolution of the gentile order in the three concrete cases of the Greek, Roman, and German nations, we may now investigate in conclusion the general economic conditions that began by undermining the gentile organization of society during the upper stage of barbarism and ended by doing away with it entirely at the advent of civilization. Marx's "Capital" will be as necessary for the successful completion of this task as Morgan's "Ancient Society."

A growth of the middle stage and a product of further development during the upper stage of savagery, the gens reached its prime, as near as we can judge from our sources of information, in the lower stage of barbarism. With this stage, then, we begin our investigation.

In our standard example, the American redskins of that time, we find the gentile constitution fully developed. A tribe had differentiated into several gentes, generally two. Through the increase of the population, these original gentes again divided into several daughter gentes, making the mother gens a phratry. The tribe itself split up into several tribes, in each of which we again meet a large number of representatives of the old gentes. In certain cases a federation united the related tribes. This simple organization fully sufficed for the social conditions out of which it had grown. It was nothing else than the innate, spontaneous expression of those conditions, and it was well calculated to smooth over all internal difficulties that could arise in this social

THE ORIGIN OF THE FAMILY

organization. External difficulties were settled by war. Such a war could end in the annihilation of a tribe, but never in its subjugation. It is the grandeur and at the same time the limitation of the gentile order that it has no room either for masters or servants. There were as yet no distinctions between rights and duties. The question whether he had a right to take part in public affairs, to practice blood revenge or to demand atonement for injuries would have appeared as absurd to an Indian, as the question whether it was his duty to eat, sleep, and hunt. Nor could any division of a tribe or gens into different classes take place. This leads us to the investigation of the economic basis of those conditions.

The population was very small in numbers. It was collected only on the territory of the tribe. Next to this territory was the hunting ground surrounding it in a wide circle. A neutral forest formed the line of demarcation from other tribes. The division of labor was quite primitive. The work was simply divided between the two sexes. The men went to war, hunted, fished, provided the raw material for food and the tools necessary for these pursuits. The women cared for the house, and prepared food and clothing; they cooked, weaved and sewed. Each sex was master of its own field of activity; the men in the forest, the women in the house. Each sex also owned the tools made and used by it; the men were the owners of the weapons, of the hunting and fishing tackle, the women of the household goods and utensils. The household was communistic, comprising several, and often many, families.* Whatever

Author's note.
*Especially on the northwest coast of America; see Bancroft. Among the Haidahs of the Queen Charlotte Islands some households gather as many as 700 members under one roof. Among the Nootkas whole tribes lived under one roof.

BARBARISM AND CIVILIZATION

was produced and used collectively, was regarded as common property: the house, the garden, the long boat. Here, and only here, then, do we find the "self-earned property" which jurists and economists have falsely attributed to civilized society, the last deceptive pretext of legality on which modern capitalist property is leaning.

But humanity did not everywhere remain in this stage. In Asia they found animals that could be tamed and propagated in captivity. The wild buffalo cow had to be hunted down; the tame cow gave birth to a calf once a year, and also furnished milk. Some of the most advanced tribes—Aryans, Semites, perhaps also Turanians—devoted themselves mainly to taming, and later to raising and tending, domestic animals. The segregation of cattle raising tribes from the rest of the barbarians constitutes the first great division of social labor. These stock raising tribes did not only produce more articles of food than the rest of the barbarians, but also different kinds of products. They were ahead of the others by having at their disposal not alone milk, milk products, and a greater abundance of meat, but also skins, wool, goat's hair, and the spun and woven goods which the growing abundance of the raw material brought into common use. This for the first time made a regular exchange of products possible. In former stages, exchange could only take place occasionally, and an exceptional ability in manufacturing weapons and tools may have led to a transient division of labor. For example, unquestionable remains of workshops for stone implements of the neolithic period have been found in many places. The artists who developed their ability in those shops, most probably worked for the collectivity, as did the artisans of the Indian gentile order. At any rate, no other exchange than that within the

THE ORIGIN OF THE FAMILY

tribe could exist in that stage, and even that was an exception. But after the segregation of the stock raising tribes we find all the conditions favorable to an exchange between groups of different tribes, and to a further development of this mode of trading into a fixed institution. Originally, tribe exchanged with tribe through the agency of their tribal heads. But when the herds drifted into the hands of private individuals, then the exchange between individuals prevailed more and more, until it became the established form. The principal article of exchange which the stock raising tribes offered to their neighbors was in the form of domestic animals. Cattle became the favorite commodity by which all other commodities were measured in exchange. In short, cattle assumed the functions of money and served in this capacity as early as that stage. With such necessity and rapidity was the demand for a money commodity developed at the very beginning of the exchange of commodities.

Horticulture, probably unknown to the Asiatic barbarians of the lower stage, arose not later than the middle stage of barbarism, as the forerunner of agriculture. The climate of the Turanian Highland does not admit of a nomadic life without a supply of stock feed for the long and hard winter. Hence the cultivation of meadows and grain was indispensable. The same is true of the steppes north of the Black Sea. Once grain had been grown for cattle, it soon became human food. The cultivated land belonged as yet to the tribe and was assigned first to the gens, which in its turn distributed it to the households, and finally to individuals; always for use only, not for possession. The users may have had certain claims to the land, but that was all.

Two of the industrial acquisitions of this stage are especially important. The first is the weaving

BARBARISM AND CIVILIZATION

loom, the second the melting of metal ore and the use of metals in manufacture. Copper, tin, and their alloy, bronze, were the most essential of them. Bronze furnished tools and weapons, but could not displace stone implements. Only iron could have done that, but the production of iron was as yet unknown. Gold and silver were already used for ornament and decoration, and must have been far more precious than copper and bronze.

The increase of production in all branches—stock raising, agriculture, domestic handicrafts—enabled human labor power to produce more than was necessary for its maintenance. It increased at the same time the amount of daily work that fell to the lot of every member of a gens, a household, or a single family. The addition of more labor power became desirable. It was furnished by war; the captured enemies were transformed into slaves. Under the given historical conditions, the first great division of social labor, by increasing the productivity of labor, adding to the wealth, and enlarging the field of productive activity, necessarily carried slavery in its wake. Out of the first great division of social labor arose the first great division of society into two classes: masters and servants, exploiters and exploited.

How and when the herds were transferred from the collective ownership of the tribe or gens to the proprietorship of the heads of the families, is not known to us. But it must have been practically accomplished in this stage. The herds and the other new objects of wealth brought about a revolution in the family. Procuring the means of existence had always been the man's business. The tools of production were manufactured and owned by him. The herds were the new tools of production, and their taming and tending was his work. Hence he owned the cattle and the commodities and slaves obtained in exchange for them. All the surplus now resulting from production fell to the share of the man. The woman shared in its fruition, but she could not claim its ownership. The "savage" warrior and hunter had been content to occupy the second place in the house, to give precedence to the woman. The "gentler" shepherd, standing on his wealth, assumed the first place and forced the woman back into the second place. And she had no occasion to complain. The division of labor in the family had regulated the distribution of property between man and wife. This division of labor remained unchanged. Yet the former domestic relation was now reversed, simply because the division of labor outside of the family had been altered. The same cause that once had secured the supremacy in the house for women, viz., the confining of women's activity to domestic labor, now assured the supremacy of the men in the households. The domestic labor of women was considered insignificant in comparison to men's work for a living. The latter was everything, the former a negligible quantity. At this early stage we can already see that the emancipation of women and their equality with men are impossible and remain so, as long as women are excluded from social production and restricted to domestic labor. The emancipation of women becomes feasible only then when women are enabled to take part extensively in social production, and when domestic duties require their attention in a minor degree. This state of things was brought about by the modern great industries, which not only admit of women's liberal participation in production, but actually call for it and, besides, endeavor to transform domestic work also into a public industry.

Man's advent to practical supremacy in the house-

BARBARISM AND CIVILIZATION

hold marked the removal of the last barrier to his universal supremacy. His unlimited rule was emphasized and endowed with continuity by the downfall of matriarchy, the introduction of patriarchy, and the gradual transition from the pairing family to the monogamic family. This made a breach in the old gentile order. The monogamic family became a power and lifted a threatening hand against the gens.

The next step brings us to the upper stage of barbarism, that period in which all nations of civilization go through their heroic era. It is the time of the iron sword, but also of the iron plow share and axe. The iron had become the servant of man. It is the last and most important of all raw products that play a revolutionary role in history; the last—if we except the potato.

Iron brought about agriculture on a larger scale and the clearing of extensive forest tracts for cultivation. It gave to the craftsman a tool of such hardness and sharpness that no stone, no other known metal, could withstand it. All this came about gradually. The first iron was often softer than bronze. Therefore stone implements disappeared very slowly. Not only in the Hildebrand Song, but also at Hastings in 1066, stone axes were still used in fighting. But progress was now irresistible, less interrupted and more rapid. The town, inclosing houses of stone or tiles within its turreted and crested stone walls, became the central seat of the tribe or federation of tribes. It showed an astounding progress of architecture, but also an increase of danger and of the demand for protection. Wealth increased rapidly, but it was the wealth of private individuals. Weaving, metal work and other more and more differentiating industries developed an increasing variety and display of art in produc-

THE ORIGIN OF THE FAMILY

tion. Agriculture furnished not alone grain, peas, beans and fruit, but also oil and wine, the preparation of which had now been learned. Such a diversity of action could not be displayed by any single individual. The second great division of labor took place: handicrafts separated from agriculture. The growing intensity of production and the increased productivity enhanced the value of human labor power. Slavery, which had been a rising and sporadic factor in the preceding stage, now became an essential part of the social system. The slaves ceased to be simple assistants. They were now driven in scores to the work in the fields and shops. The division of production into two great branches, agriculture and handicrafts, gave rise to production for exchange, the production of commodities. Trade arose at the same time, not only in the interior and on the tribal boundaries, but also in the form of maritime exchange. All this was as yet in a very undeveloped state. The precious metals gained preference as a universal money commodity, but still uncoined and exchanged merely by dead weight.

The distinction between rich and poor was added to that between free men and slaves. This and the new division of labor constitute a new division of society into classes. The differences in the amount of property belonging to the several family heads broke up the old communistic households one by one, wherever they might have been preserved thus far. This made an end to the collective cultivation of the soil for the account of the community. The cultivated land was assigned for use to the several families, first for a limited time, later for once and all. The transition to full private property was accomplished gradually and simultaneously with the transition from the pairing family to monogamy.

BARBARISM AND CIVILIZATION

The monogamous family began to be the economic unit of society.

The increase of population necessitated a closer consolidation against internal and external foes. The federation of related tribes became unavoidable. Their amalgamation, and thence the amalgamation of the separate tribal territories to one national territory, was the following step. The military leader—rex, basileus, thiudans—became an indispensable and standing official. The public meeting was introduced wherever it did not yet exist. The military leader, the council of chiefs, and the public meeting formed the organs of the military democracy that had grown out of the gentile constitution. Military democracy—for now war and organization for war were regular functions of social life. The wealth of the neighbors excited the greed of nations that began to regard the acquisition of wealth as one of the main purposes of their life. They were barbarians: robbing appeared to them easier and more honorable than producing. War, once simply a revenge for transgressions or a means for enlarging a territory that had become too narrow, was now waged for the sake of plunder alone and became a regular profession. Not in vain did threatening walls cast a rigid stare all around the new fortified towns: their yawning ditches were the tomb of the gentile constitution, and their turrets already reached up into civilization. The internal affairs underwent a similar change. The plundering wars increased the power of the military leader and of the subcommanders. The habitual election of the successors from the same family was gradually transformed into hereditary succession, first by sufferance, then by claim, and finally by usurpation. Thus the foundation of hereditary royalty and nobility was laid. In this manner the organs of the gentile constitution

THE ORIGIN OF THE FAMILY

were gradually torn away from their roots in the nation, tribe, phratry and gens, and the whole gentile order reversed into its antithesis. The organization of tribes for the purpose of the free administration of affairs was turned into an organization for plundering and oppressing their neighbors. The organs of gentilism changed from servants of the public will to independent organs of rule oppressing their own people. This could not have happened, if the greed for wealth had not divided the gentiles into rich and poor; if the "difference of property in a gens had not changed the community of interest into antagonism of the gentiles" (Karl Marx); and if the extension of slavery had not begun by branding work for a living as slavish and more ignominious than plundering.

We have now reached the threshold of civilization. This stage is inaugurated by a new progress in the division of labor. In the lower stage of barbarism production was carried on for use only; any acts of exchange were confined to single cases when a surplus was accidentally realized. In the middle stage of barbarism we find that the possession of cattle gave a regular surplus to the nomadic nations with sufficiently large herds. At the same time there was a division of labor between nomadic nations and backward nations without herds. The existence of two different stages of production side by side furnished the conditions necessary for a regular exchange. The upper stage of barbarism introduced a new division of labor between agriculture and handicrafts, resulting in the production of a continually increasing amount of commodities for the special purpose of exchange, so that exchange between individuals became a vital function of society. Civilization strengthened and intensified all the established

BARBARISM AND CIVILIZATION

divisions of labor, especially by rendering the contrast between city and country more pronounced. Either the town may have the economic control over the country, as during antiquity, or vice versa, as in the middle ages. A third division of labor was added by civilization: it created a class that did not take part in production, but occupied itself merely with the exchange of products—the merchants. All former attempts at class formation were exclusively concerned with production. They divided the producers into directors and directed, or into producers on a more or less extensive scale. But here a class appears for the first time that captures the control of production in general and subjugates the producers to its rule, without taking the least part in production. A class that makes itself the indispensable mediator between two producers and exploits them both under the pretext of saving them the trouble and risk of exchange, of extending the markets for their products to distant regions, and of thus becoming the most useful class in society; a class of parasites, genuine social ichneumons, that skim the cream off production at home and abroad as a reward for very insignificant services; that rapidly amass enormous wealth and gain social influence accordingly; that for this reason reap ever new honors and ever greater control of production during the period of civilization, until they at last bring to light a product of their own—periodical crises in industry.

At the stage of production under discussion, our young merchant class had no inkling as yet of the great future that was in store for them. But they continued to organize, to make themselves invaluable, and that was sufficient for the moment. At the same time metal coins came into use, and through them a new device for controlling the producers and their products. The commodity of commodities that was hiding all other commodities in its mysterious bosom had been discovered, a charm that could be transformed at will into any desirable or coveted thing. Whoever held it in his possession had the world of production at his command. And who had it above all others? The merchant. In his hands the cult of money was safe. He took care to make it plain that all commodities, and hence all producers, must prostrate themselves in adoration before money. He proved by practice that all other forms of wealth are reduced to thin wraiths before this personification of riches. Never again did the power of money show itself in such primordial brutality and violence as in its youthful days. After the sale of commodities for money came the borrowing of money, resulting in interest and usury. And no legislation of any later period stretches the debtor so mercilessly at the feet of the speculating creditor as the antique Grecian and Roman codes—both of them spontaneous products of habit, without any other than economic pressure.

The wealth in commodities and slaves was now further increased by large holdings in land. The titles of the individuals to the lots of land formerly assigned to them by the gens or tribe had become so well established, that these lots were now owned and inherited. What the individuals had most desired of late was the liberation from the claim of the gentiles to their lots, a claim which had become a veritable fetter for them. They were rid of this fetter—but soon after they were also rid of their lots. The full, free ownership of the soil implied not only the possibility of uncurtailed possession, but also of selling the soil. As long as the soil belonged to the gens, this was impossible. But when the new land owner shook off the chains of the priority claim of the gens and tribe, he also tore the bond that had so

BARBARISM AND CIVILIZATION

long tied him indissolubly to the soil. What that meant was impressed on him by the money invented simultaneously with the advent of private property in land. The soil could now become a commodity to be bought and sold. Hardly had private ownership of land been introduced, when the mortgage put in its appearance (see Athens). As hetaerism and prostitution clung to the heels of monogamy, so does from now on the mortgage to private ownership in land. You have clamored for free, full, saleable land. Well, then, there you have it—tu l'as voulu, Georges Dandin; it was your own wish, George Dandin.

Industrial expansion, money, usury, private land, and mortgage thus progressed with the concentration and centralization of wealth in the hands of a small class, accompanied by the increasing impoverishment of the masses and the increasing mass of paupers. The new aristocracy of wealth, so far as it did not coincide with the old tribal nobility, forced the latter permanently into the background (in Athens, in Rome, among the Germans). And this division of free men into classes according to their wealth was accompanied, especially in Greece, by an enormous increase in the number of slaves * whose forced labor formed the basis on which the whole superstructure of society was reared.

Let us now see what became of the gentile constitution through this revolution of society. Gentilism stood powerless in the face of the new elements that had grown without its assistance. It was dependent on the condition that the members of a gens, or of a tribe, should live together in the same territory and be its exclusive inhabitants. That had long ceased

---

Author's note.
*The number of slaves in Athens was 365,000. In Corinth it was 460,000 at the most flourishing time, and 470,000 in Aegina; in both cases ten times the number of free citizens.

THE ORIGIN OF THE FAMILY

to be the case. Gentes and tribes were everywhere hopelessly intermingled, slaves, clients, and foreigners lived among citizens. The capacity for settling down permanently which had only been acquired near the end of the middle stage of barbarism, was time and again sidetracked by the necessity of changing the abode according to the dictates of commerce, different occupations and the transfer of land. The members of the gentile organizations could no longer meet for the purpose of taking care of their common interests. Only matters of little importance, such as religious festivals, were still observed in an indifferent way. Beside the wants and interests for the care of which the gentile organs were appointed and fitted, new wants and interests had arisen from the revolution of the conditions of existence and the resulting change in social classification. These new wants and interests were not only alien to the old gentile order, but thwarted it in every way. The interests of the craftsmen created by division of labor, and the special necessities of a town differing from those of the country, required new organs. But every one of these groups was composed of people from different gentes, phratries, and tribes; they included even strangers. Hence the new organs necessarily had to form outside of the gentile constitution. But by the side of it meant against it. And again, in every gentile organization the conflict of interests made itself felt and reached its climax by combining rich and poor, usurers and debtors, in the same gens and tribe. There was furthermore the mass of inhabitants who were strangers to the gentiles. These strangers could become very powerful, as in Rome, and they were too numerous to be gradually absorbed by the gentes and tribes. The gentiles confronted these masses as a compact body of privileged individuals. What had once been a nat-

BARBARISM AND CIVILIZATION

ural democracy, had been transformed into an odious aristocracy. The gentile constitution had grown out of a society that did not know any internal contradictions, and it was only adapted to such a society. It had no coërcive power except public opinion. But now a society had developed that by force of all its economic conditions of existence divided humanity into freemen and slaves, and exploiting rich and exploited poor. A society that not only could never reconcile these contradictions, but drove them ever more to a climax. Such a society could only exist by a continual open struggle of all classes against one another, or under the supremacy of a third power that under a pretense of standing above the struggling classes stifled their open conflict and permitted a class struggle only on the economic field, in a so-called "legal" form. Gentilism had ceased to live. It was crushed by the division of labor and by its result, the division of society into classes. It was replaced by the State.

In preceding chapters we have shown by three concrete examples the three main forms in which the state was built up on the ruins of gentilism. Athens represented the simplest, the classic type: the state grew directly and mainly out of class divisions that developed within gentile society. In Rome the gentile organization became an exclusive aristocracy amid a numerous plebs of outsiders who had only duties, but no rights. The victory of the plebs burst the old gentile order asunder and erected on its remains the state which soon engulfed both gentile aristocracy and plebs. Finally, among the German conquerors of the Roman empire, the state grew as a direct result of the conquest of large foreign territories which the gentile constitution was powerless to control. But this conquest did not necessitate either

THE ORIGIN OF THE FAMILY

a serious fight with the former population or a more advanced division of labor. Conquerors and conquered were almost in the same stage of economic development, so that the economic basis of society remained undisturbed. Hence gentilism could preserve for many centuries an unchanged territorial character in the form of mark communes, and even rejuvenate itself in the nobility and patrician families of later years, or in the peasantry, as e. g. in Dithmarsia.*

The state, then, is by no means a power forced on society from outside; neither is it the "realization of the ethical idea," "the image and the realization of reason," as Hegel maintains. It is simply a product of society at a certain stage of evolution. It is the confession that this society has become hopelessly divided against itself, has entangled itself in irreconcilable contradictions which it is powerless to banish. In order that these contradictions, these classes with conflicting economic interests, may not annihilate themselves and society in a useless struggle, a power becomes necessary that stands apparently above society and has the function of keeping down the conflicts and maintaining "order." And this power, the outgrowth of society, but assuming supremacy over it and becoming more and more divorced from it, is the state.

The state differs from gentilism in that it first divides its members by territories. As we have seen, the old bonds of blood kinship uniting the gentile bodies had become inefficient, because they were dependent on the condition, now no longer a fact, that all gentiles should live on a certain territory. The

---

Author's note.
*The first historian who had at least a vague conception of the nature of the gens was Niebuhr, thanks to his familiarity with the Dithmarsian families. The same source, however, is also responsible for his errors.

BARBARISM AND CIVILIZATION

territory was the same; but the human beings had changed. Hence the division by territories was chosen as the point of departure, and citizens had to exercise their rights and duties wherever they chose their abode without regard to gens and tribe. This organization of inhabitants by localities is a common feature of all states. It seems natural to us now. But we have seen what long and hard fighting was required before it could take, in Athens and Rome, the place of the old organization by blood kinship.

In the second place, the state created a public power of coërcion that did no longer coincide with the old self-organized and armed population. This special power of coërcion is necessary, because a self-organized army of the people has become impossible since the division of society into classes took place. For the slaves belonged also to society. The 90,000 citizens of Athens formed only a privileged class compared to the 365,000 slaves. The popular army of the Athenian democracy was an aristocratic public power designed to keep the slaves down. But we have seen that a police force became also necessary to maintain order among the citizens. This public power of coërcion exists in every state. It is not composed of armed men alone, but has also such objects as prisons and correction houses attached to it, that were unknown to gentilism. It may be very small, almost infinitesimal, in societies with feebly developed class antagonisms and in out of the way places, as was once the case in certain regions of the United States. But it increases in the same ratio in which the class antagonisms become more pronounced, and in which neighboring states become larger and more populous. A conspicuous example is modern Europe, where the class struggles and wars of conquest have nursed the public power to such a size that it threatens to swallow the whole society and the state itself.

THE ORIGIN OF THE FAMILY

In order to maintain this public power, contributions of the citizens become necessary—the taxes. These were absolutely unknown in gentile society. But today we get our full measure of them. As civilization makes further progress, these taxes are no longer sufficient to cover public expenses. The state makes drafts on the future, contracts loans, public debts. Old Europe can tell a story of them.

In possession of the public power and of the right of taxation, the officials in their capacity as state organs are now exalted above society. The free and voluntary respect that was accorded to the organs of gentilism does not satisfy them any more, even if they might have it. Representatives of a power that is divorced from society, they must enforce respect by exceptional laws that render them specially sacred and inviolable.* The lowest police employee of the civilized state has more "authority" than all the organs of gentilism combined. But the mightiest prince and the greatest statesman or general of civilization may look with envy on the spontaneous and undisputed esteem that was the privilege of the least gentile sachem. The one stands in the middle of society, the other is forced to assume a position outside and above it.

The state is the result of the desire to keep down class conflicts. But having arisen amid these conflicts, it is as a rule the state of the most powerful economic class that by force of its economic supremacy becomes also the ruling political class and thus acquires new means of subduing and exploiting the oppressed masses. The antique state was, therefore, the state of the slave owners for the purpose of hold-

---

Translator's note.
*The recent demand for a law declaring the person of the U. S. President sacred above all other representatives of the public power and making an assault on him an exceptional crime is a very good case in point.

BARBARISM AND CIVILIZATION

ing the slaves in check. The feudal state was the organ of the nobility for the oppression of the serfs and dependent farmers. The modern representative state is the tool of the capitalist exploiters of wage labor. At certain periods it occurs exceptionally that the struggling classes balance each other so nearly that the public power gains a certain degree of independence by posing as the mediator between them. The absolute monarchy of the seventeenth and eighteenth century was in such a position, balancing the nobles and the burghers against one another. So was the Bonapartism of the first, and still more of the second, empire, playing the proletariat against the bourgeoisie and vice versa. The latest performance of this kind, in which ruler and ruled appear equally ridiculous, is the new German empire of Bismarckian make, in which capitalists and laborers are balanced against one another and equally cheated for the benefit of the degenerate Prussian cabbage junkers.*

In most of the historical states, the rights of the citizens are differentiated according to their wealth. This is a direct confirmation of the fact that the state is organized for the protection of the possessing against the non-possessing classes. The Athenian and Roman classification by incomes shows this. It is also seen in the medieval state of feudalism in which the political power depended on the quantity of real estate. It is again seen in the electoral qualifications of the modern representative state. The political recognition of the differences in wealth is by no means essential. On the contrary, it marks a low stage of state development. The highest form of the state, the democratic republic, knows officially noth-

---
Translator's note.
*"Junker" is a contemptuous term for the land-owning nobility.

THE ORIGIN OF THE FAMILY

ing of property distinctions.* It is that form of the state which under modern conditions of society becomes more and more an unavoidable necessity. The last decisive struggle between proletariat and bourgeoisie can only be fought out under this state form.* In such a state, wealth exerts its power indirectly, but all the more safely. This is done partly in the form of direct corruption of officials, after the classical type of the United States, or in the form of an alliance between government and bankers which is established all the more easily when the public debt increases and when corporations concentrate in their hands not only the means of transportation, but also production itself, using the stock exchange as a center. The United States and the latest French republic are striking examples, and good old Switzerland has contributed its share to illustrate this point. That a democratic republic is not necessary for this fraternal bond between stock exchange and government is proved by England and last, not least, Germany, where it is doubtful whether Bismarck or Bleichroeder was more favored by the introduction of universal suffrage.* The possessing class rules

---

Translator's note.

*In the United States, the poll tax is an indirect property qualification, as it strikes those who, through lack of employment, sickness or invalidity, are unable to spare the amount, however small, of this tax. Furthermore, the laws requiring a continuous residence in the precinct, the town, the county, and the State as a qualification for voters have the effect of disqualifying a great number of workingmen who are forced to change their abode according to their opportunities for employment. And the educational qualifications which especially the Southern States are rigidly enforcing tend to disfranchise the great mass of the negroes, who form the main body of the working class in those States. Translator's note.

*In Belgium, where the proletariat is now on the verge of gaining political supremacy, the battle cry is: "S. U. et R. P." (Suffrage Universelle et Representation Proportionelle). Translator's note.

*Suffrage in Germany, though universal for men is by no

BARBARISM AND CIVILIZATION

directly through universal suffrage. For as long as the oppressed class, in this case the proletariat, is not ripe for its economic emancipation, just so long will its majority regard the existing order of society as the only one possible, and form the tail, the extreme left wing, of the capitalist class. But the more the proletariat matures toward its self-emancipation, the more does it constitute itself as a separate class and elect its own representatives in place of the capitalists. Universal suffrage is the gauge of the maturity of the working class. It can and will never be anything else but that in the modern state. But that is sufficient. On the day when the thermometer of universal suffrage reaches its boiling point among the laborers, they as well as the capitalists will know what to do.

The state, then, did not exist from all eternity. There have been societies without it, that had no idea of any state or public power. At a certain stage of economic development, which was of necessity accompanied by a division of society into classes, the state became the inevitable result of this division. We are now rapidly approaching a stage of evolution in production, in which the existence of classes has not only ceased to be a necessity, but becomes a positive fetter on production. Hence these classes must fall as inevitably as they once arose. The state must irrevocably fall with them. The society that is to reorganize production on the basis of a free and equal association of the producers, will transfer the machinery of state where it will then belong: into the

---

means equal, but founded on property qualifications. In Prussia, e. g., a three class system of voting is in force which is best illustrated by the following figures: In 1898 there were 6,447,253 voters; 3.26 per cent belonged to the first class, 11.51 per cent to the second class, and 85.35 per cent to the third class. But the 947,218 voters of the first and second classes had twice as many votes as the five and a half millions of the third class.

THE ORIGIN OF THE FAMILY

Museum of Antiquities by the side of the spinning wheel and the bronze ax.

Civilization is, as we have seen, that stage of society, in which the division of labor, the resulting exchange between individuals, and the production of commodities combining them, reach their highest development and revolutionize the whole society.

The production of all former stages of society was mainly collective, and consumption was carried on by direct division of products within more or less small communes. This collective production was confined within the narrowest limits. But it implied the control of production and of the products by the producers. They knew what became of their product: it did not leave their hands until it was consumed by them. As long as production moved on this basis, it could not grow beyond the control of the producers, and it could not create any strange ghostly forces against them. Under civilization, however, this is the inevitable rule.

Into the simple process of production, the division of labor was gradually interpolated. It undermined the communism of production and consumption, it made the appropriation of products by single individuals the prevailing rule, and thus introduced the exchange between individuals, in the manner mentioned above. Gradually, the production of commodities became the rule.

This mode of production for exchange, not for home consumption, necessarily passes the products on from hand to hand. The producer gives his product away in exchange. He does no longer know what becomes of it. With the advent of money and of the trader who steps in as a middleman between the producers, the process of exchange becomes still more complicated. The fate of the products becomes still more

BARBARISM AND CIVILIZATION

uncertain. The number of merchants is great and one does not know what the other is doing. The products now pass not only from hand to hand, but also from market to market. The producers have lost the control of the aggregate production in their sphere of life, and the merchants have not yet acquired this control. Products and production become the victims of chance. But chance is only one pole of an interrelation, the other pole of which is called necessity. In nature, where chance seems to reign also, we have long ago demonstrated the innate necessity and law that determines the course of chance on every line. But what is true of nature, holds also good of society. Whenever a social function or a series of social processes become too powerful for the control of man, whenever they grow beyond the grasp of man and seem to be left to mere chance, then the peculiar and innate laws of such processes shape the course of chance with increased elementary necessity. Such laws also control the vicissitudes of the production and exchange of commodities. For the individual producer and exchanger, these laws are strange, and often unknown, forces, the nature of which must be laboriously investigated and ascertained. These economic laws of production are modified by the different stages of this form of production. But generally speaking, the entire period of civilization is dominated by these laws. To this day, the product controls the producer. To this day, the aggregate production of society is managed, not on a uniform plan, but by blind laws, that rule with elementary force and find their final expression in the storms of periodical commercial crises.

We have seen that human labor power is enabled at a very early stage of production to produce considerably more than is needed to maintain the pro-

THE ORIGIN OF THE FAMILY

ducer. We have found that this stage coincided in general with the first appearance of the division of labor and of exchange between individuals. Now, it was not long before the great truth was discovered that man may himself be a commodity, and that human labor power may be exchanged and exploited by transforming a man into a slave. Hardly had exchange between men been established, when men themselves were also exchanged. The active asset bcame a passive liability, whether man wanted it or not.

Slavery, which reaches its highest development in civilization, introduced the first great division of an exploited and an exploiting class into society. This division continued during the whole period of civilization. Slavery is the first form of exploitation, characteristic of the antique world. Then followed feudalism in the middle ages, and wage labor in recent times. These are the three great forms of servitude, characteristic of the three great epochs of civilization. Their invariable mark is either open or, in modern times, disguised slavery.

The stage of commodity production introducing civilization is marked economically by the introduction of (1) metal coins and, thus, of money as capital, of interest, and of usury; (2) merchants as middlemen between producers; (3) private property and mortgage; (4) slave labor as the prevailing form of production. The form of the family corresponding to civilization and becoming its pronounced custom is monogamy, the supremacy of man over woman, and the monogamous family as the economic unit of society. The aggregation of civilized society is the state, which throughout all typical periods is the state of the ruling class, and in all cases mainly a machine for controlling the oppressed and exploited class. Civilization is furthermore characterized on one side by

BARBARISM AND CIVILIZATION

the permanent introduction of the contrast between city and country as the basis of the entire division of social labor; on the other side by the introduction of the testament by which the property holder is enabled to dispose of his property beyond the hour of his death. This institution is a direct blow at the gentile constitution, and was unknown in Athens until the time of Solon. In Rome it was introduced very early, but we do not know when.* In Germany it was originated by the priests in order that the honest German might bequeath his property to the church without any interference.

With this fundamental constitution, civilization had accomplished things for which the old gentile society was no match whatever. But these exploits were accomplished by playing on the most sordid passions and instincts of man, and by developing them at the expense of all his other gifts. Barefaced covetousness was the moving spirit of civilization from its first dawn to the present day; wealth, and again wealth, and for the third time wealth; wealth, not of society, but of the puny individual, was its only and final aim. If nevertheless the advanced development of science, and at repeated times the highest flower of art, fell into its lap, this was only due to the fact

---

Author's note.

*Lassalle's "System of Acquired Rights" argues in its second part mainly the proposition that the Roman testament is as old as Rome itself, and that there has never been in Roman history "a time without a testament." According to him, the testament had its origin in pre-Roman times in the cult of the departed. Lassalle, as a convinced Hegelian of the old school, derives the provisions of the Roman law, not from the social condition of the Romans, but from the "speculative conception" of will, and thus arrives at this totally anti-historic conclusion. This is not to be wondered at in a book that draws from the same speculative conception the conclusion that the transfer of property was purely a side issue in Roman inheritance. Lassalle not only believed in the illusions of Roman jurists,. especially of the earlier ones, but he outstripped their fancy.

THE ORIGIN OF THE FAMILY

that without them the highest emoluments of modern wealth would have been missing. Exploitation of one class by another being the basis of civilization, its whole development involves a continual contradiction. Every progress of production is at the same time a retrogression in the condition of the oppressed class, that is of the great majority. Every benefit for one class is necessarily an evil for the other, every new emancipation of one class a new oppression for the other. The most drastic proof of this is furnished by the introduction of machinery, the effects of which are well known to-day. And while there is hardly any distinction between rights and duties among barbarians, as we have seen, civilization makes the difference between these two plain even to the dullest mind. For now one class has nearly all the rights, the other class nearly all the duties.

But this is not admitted. What is good for the ruling class, is alleged to be good for the whole of society with which the ruling class identifies itself. The more civilization advances, the more it is found to cover with the cloak of charity the evils necessarily created by it, to excuse them or to deny their existence, in short to introduce a conventional hypocrisy that culminates in the declaration: The exploitation of the oppressed class is carried on by the exploiting class solely in the interest of the exploited class itself. And if the latter does not recognize this, but even becomes rebellious, it is simply the worst ingratitude to its benefactors, the exploiters.*

Author's note.

*I first intended to place the brilliant critique of civilization, scattered through the works of Fourier, by the side of Morgan's and of my own. Unluckily I cannot spare the time. I only wish to remark that Fourier already considers monogamy and private property in land the main characteristics of civilization, and that he calls them a war of the

BARBARISM AND CIVILIZATION

And now, in conclusion, let me add Morgan's judgment of civilization (Ancient Society, page 552):

"Since the advent of civilization, the outgrowth of property has been so immense, its forms so diversified, its uses so expanding and its management so intelligent in the interest of its owners that it has become, on the part of the people, an unmanageable power. The human mind stands bewildered in the presence of its own creation. The time will come nevertheless, when human intelligence will rise to the mastery over property, and define the relations of the state to the property it protects, as well as the obligations and the limits of the rights of its owners. The interests of society are paramount to individual interests, and the two must be brought into just and harmonious relations. A mere property career is not the final destiny of mankind, if progress is to be the law of the future as it has been of the past. The time which has passed away since civilization began is but a fragment of the past duration of man's existence; and but a fragment of the ages yet to come. The dissolution of society bids fair to become the termination of a career of which property is the end and aim, because such a career contains the elements of self-destruction. Democracy in government, brotherhood in society, equality in rights and privileges, and universal education, foreshadow the next higher plane of society to which experience, intelligence and knowledge are steadily tending. It will be a revival, in a higher form, of the liberty, equality and fraternity of the ancient gentes."

---

rich against the poor. We also find with him the deep perception that the individual families (les familles incoherentes) are the economic units of all faulty societies divided by opposing interests.

THE END.